CIMA P3

Risk Management

Course Notes

Copyright © 2015 Strategic Business Coaching Ltd

All rights reserved. Personal use only - not licensed for use on courses. Any unauthorised copying or sharing of this material is punishable by CIMA under the CIMA code of ethics

First published in 2014

ISBN-13:9781505224993
ISBN-10:1505224993

www.astranti.com

Chapter 1 7
Risk 7

    1. Risk 8
    2. Types of risk 8
    3. Strategic Business risks 9
    4. Operational business risks 12
    5. Financial risk 13
    6. International risks 14
    7. Attitudes to risk 16
    8. Human decision making and risk 16

Chapter 2 19
Risk Management 19

    1. Risk Management 20
    2. Principles of good risk management 21
    3. Risk Management Process 23
    4. Gross vs Net Risks 30
    5. Enterprise risk management (ERM) – COSO 32
    6. CIMA's Risk Management Cycle 34
    7. Problems of risk management 35
    8. Assurance mapping 36
    9. Risk register 37

Chapter 3 39
Governance and Reporting 39

    1. Governance 40
    2. Principles of corporate governance 41
    3. The UK Code of Corporate Governance 42
    4. Committees responsible for risk management 45
    5. Director's pay and governance 46
    6. Key governance risks 47
    7. Risk Reporting 48

Chapter 4 51
Internal Control 51

    1. Internal Control 52
    2. Key features of internal control systems 53
    3. Role of key stakeholders in control 54
    4. Control objectives 56
    5. Control activities or procedures 57
    6. Levels of control 58
    7. Control precision and sufficiency 58
    8. Control weaknesses and compliance failures 59
    9. Internal control and Fraud 61
    10. Problems with internal control 62

Chapter 5 65
Management Control Systems 65

    1. Management control systems 66
    2. Management control 66
    3. Management accounting control systems 71
    4. Controlling Ethics 73
    5. CIMA Code of ethics 76
    6. Controlling Quality 78
    7. Lean Production and Management 80
    8. Controls by department 82
    9. Risks in control systems 84

Chapter 6..87
Performance measurement..87
1. Control theory, performance targets and feedback.............................88
2. Types of responsibility centres..90
3. Performance measurement of responsibility centres..........................91
4. Balanced Scorecard..96
5. Transfer pricing..98
6. Calculating a transfer price..99
7. Other considerations in transfer pricing...109
8. Transfer pricing summary...111

Chapter 7..113
Controlling Information Systems..113
1. The importance of IT..114
2. Information strategies..114
3. Managing the IS department...116
4. Steering committee..117
5. Big data...117
6. Systems development...120
7. IT controls...122

Chapter 8..125
Internal Auditing...125
1. Internal auditing..126
2. Developing the audit plans..127
3. Undertaking an internal audit..129
4. Analytical review..130
5. Computer-assisted audit techniques..133
6. Internal audit reports...133
7. Effective internal audit...134
8. Role in corporate governance...136
9. Relationship with the external auditor..137

Chapter 9..139
Financial Risk...139
1. What is financial risk?..140
2. Investment risks...140
3. Financial risks associated with international operations.................141
4. Quantifying risk..143
5. Diversification..145
6. Treasury department and financial risk..146

Chapter 10..147
Currency Risk..147
1. Currency risk..148
2. Translation risk..148
3. Transaction risk...148
4. Exchange rates terminology...149
5. Interest rate parity theory..150
6. Purchasing power parity theory..151

Chapter 11...153
Currency hedging techniques...153
   1. Hedging and Transaction Risk..154
   2. Forwards...155
   3. Money market hedge..157
   4. Currency futures..160
   5. Currency options..162
   6. Currency SWAPS...163

Chapter 12...165
Interest rate risk...165
   1. Interest rate risk..166
   2. Hedging interest rate risk..166
   3. Interest rate SWAPS..168
   4. Caps, Floors and Collars..170

Chapter 13...171
Investment Appraisal Risk..171
   1. Investment appraisal risks..172
   2. Sensitivity Analysis...174
   3. Certainty Equivalents..175
   4. Diversification and systematic risk...176
   5. Capital asset pricing model..177
   6. Adjusted present value...180
   7. Project implementation and review...182

CIMA P3 Course Notes

Chapter 1
Risk

1. Risk

What is risk?

So, you are going out shopping. As you do that you are taking a whole range of risks – the risk of being overcharged, the risk of buying something you won't use, the risk of being in an accident on the way there or back, the risk you'll meet a friend and get held up chatting and miss an appointment and so on. In fact we could just go on an on, listing out all the things that could go wrong – and that is the essence of risk.

Here's the definition then.....

Risk is the potential that a chosen action will lead to an undesirable outcome.

In business too the number of things that could 'lead to an undesirable outcome' are endless, but they must be understood and managed by the business. Ultimately commercial risks result in a negative outcome in terms of some business goal – an increase in costs, fall in revenues, loss of customers, legal liability, drop in morale of staff and so on.

Upside vs Downside risk

Now our general definition above actually relates to **'downside risk'** which is when things go wrong. Occasionally you may also see a broader definition of risk being anything which varies from expectation when we can also then see the term **'upside risk'** that being the risk that something positive happens. The risk that we turn up at the supermarket and there's a sale on that saves us lots of money, for instance.

Downside risk is typically the focus for risk management, after all we're usually quite happy to take any upsides and don't therefore need to 'manage them'. Upside risk is something you'll see dealt with only vary rarely throughout these notes, and from now on you can usually assume that when we talk about 'risk' we're talking about downside risk unless we say otherwise.

2. Types of risk

Risks can be categorised into different groups to help understand and manage risk better.

The main categories of risk to consider are:

Strategic – relating to the business and its strategic position, for example a new competitor entering the market, challenging the company's competitive position and affecting their ability to earn revenues and profits.

Compliance - with law and regulation, for example health and safety legislation

Financial – risks relating to financing the business (such as changing interest rates) and undertaking financial transactions (such as exchange rate risk or non-payment by a customer)

Operational – risk in undertaking day to day business - for example the breakdown or theft of key equipment

These categories are not rigid and some risks may fall into more than one category. The risks attached to data protection could be related to both operations and compliance for instance.

Risk categorisation can help manage risks effectively:

- to help **identify risks**, which can be done in more detail in smaller categories than when looking at the organisation as a whole. The four categories above would typically be split down into many smaller sub-categories to help this process.

- to **analyse the risks** better as specialists in a particular area might be best qualified to examine risks related to that area. For example the finance team would be in the best position to identify key financial risks.

- to decide who is best **taking responsibility** for managing those risks, with, for instance the directors managing the strategic risks and the finance department the financial risks.

3. Strategic Business risks

Strategic risk relates to the business and its strategic position. They are typically managed by the board of directors as part of their remit to set and manage the strategy of the business.

A good starting point is to consider risks arising under the PESTEL factors which are **key sources of external risks**:

Political risk

Political factors are how and to what degree a government intervenes in the workings of organisations. Political factors include areas such as tax policy, employment legislation, environmental laws, trade restrictions, tariffs, and political stability.

Government investment (or lack of) can also play a significant role in the availability of contracts and work for organisations. Governments have great influence on the health, education, and infrastructure of a nation which can also impact the organisations within that country e.g. the availability of skilled labour or funding availability within particular sectors.

Political changes therefore create significant risks for organisations within that country.

Economic risk

Economic factors include economic growth, interest rates, exchange rates and the inflation rate. These factors have major impacts on how businesses operate and make decisions. For example, interest rates affect a firm's cost of capital and therefore to what extent a business grows and expands. Exchange rates affect the costs of exporting goods and the supply and price of imported goods in an economy.

Economic change therefore creates risk for organisations within that economy.

Social risk

Social factors include the cultural aspects and include health consciousness, population growth rate, age distribution, career attitudes and emphasis on safety. Trends in social factors affect the demand for a company's products and how that company operates.

Social change can therefore create risk, for example the reduction in demand for unhealthy products as health consciousness increases.

Technological risk

Technological factors include IT, the internet, social media, automation, and the rate of technological change. Organisations need to stay aware of the key technologies in their industry in order to manage risks that they do not fully adapt to or apply new technologies.

Environmental risk

Environmental factors include ecological and environmental aspects such as weather, climate, and climate change, which may especially affect industries such as tourism, farming, and insurance.

Furthermore, growing awareness of the potential impacts of climate change is affecting how companies operate and the products they offer, both creating new markets and diminishing or destroying existing ones.

Environmental risks can apply to longer term changes that affect markets (e.g. climate change) or short term activities such as a one-off pollution event.

Legal risk

Changes in law can include impacts on products, customers, staff, and product demand. Companies must continue to keep aware of legal changes to avoid the risk that they do not abide by the law which could result in fines and damage to their reputation.

Our next set of risks to consider can be related to the elements of Porter's 5 forces, a business strategy model which examines the key issues at an industry level (e.g. the oil industry, supermarket industry, banking industry and so on):

Competitive risks

These factors relate to changes caused by competitors in the market. They include new or changing products, price changes, new distribution channels, branding and market positioning.

Risk of new entrants

Are new competitors likely to be entering the industry and what impact would they have if they did?

Supplier risk

Supplier factors include changing prices, availability and reliability of supply, delays in delivery, quality issues. As well as increases in costs imposed by changes in supply, supply factors create risk of poor customer service and ultimately affect the company's reputation and profitability.

Customer risk

Customers may move to other competitors or exert power to reduce prices. Key customers may also cease to exist, for instance when a business goes into liquidation. Over dependence on a small number of key customers is a major risk of many businesses.

Risk of substitute products

A substitute is a product that fulfils the same need as the product a company produces. Professional football clubs might see cricket, rugby, basketball, golf and tennis as substitute products. There is a risk that a substitute product will become popular and reduce demand for the company's product. For example email has taken over from fax machines as the method of immediate document transmission, and fax machine manufacturers would have needed to have been aware of this risk and its effect during the decline of that market.

4. Operational business risks

Key operational risks

Operational risks are internal risks, relating to the day to day functioning of the business.

These can include:

- IT systems breakdown, error or failure
- Loss or corruption of data
- Legal and regulatory compliance
- Health and safety issues
- Loss of key staff
- Increasing wages
- Shortages of skilled staff
- Fraud
- Human error
- Damage, loss or theft of assets.

Risk and large projects

Due to the very wide variety of opportunities for problems in large projects such as large construction projects or IT developments these are often highly risky. Such ventures typically have high cost overruns, benefit shortfalls where initial objectives are not fully achieved, and delays.

Research suggests that cost overruns of 50% are common on large projects, while actual demand for the end services they are planned to provide is commonly 25% less than anticipated.

Large projects therefore need very clear, detailed feasibility analysis at the project inception, and strong project management throughout the project.

5. Financial risk

Definition

Financial risks relate to:

- financing the business (such as changing interest rates or non-availability of finance)

- undertaking financial transactions (such as exchange rate risk or non-payment by a customer (credit risk))

- the possibility that an investment's actual return will be different than expected. This includes the possibility of losing some or all of the original investment.

- Insufficient cashflow, so there is not enough cash to pay suppliers or interest payments.

- Credit risk: customers do not pay, resulting in bad debts.

Financial risk may be market-dependent, determined by numerous market factors such as the changing economy, or operational, resulting from error or fraudulent behaviour.

Measuring financial risk of investments

Financial risk often includes not only "downside risk" but also "upside risk" (returns that exceed expectations). **Standard deviation** is the calculation of the variability of returns around the mean, and provides a measure of financial risk. (You will not be required to undertake a standard deviation calculation for the exam where questions tend to focus on the downside rather than the upside risk.)

Risk and return

A fundamental idea in finance is the relationship between risk and return. The greater the potential return one might seek, the greater the risk that one generally assumes.

For example, a government bond (effectively making a loan to the government) is considered to be one of the safest investments and, when compared to a corporate bond (effectively loaning to a company), provides a lower rate of return. The reason for this is that a corporation is much more likely to go bankrupt than a government. Because the risk of investing in a corporate bond is higher, investors are offered a higher rate of return.

6. International risks

Risks tend to widen when organisations are operating internationally.

Again the PESTEL factors are a good starting point to assess risk.

Political – International politics, uncertainty and war. The political situation in each market operated needs to be considered.

Economic – World economy. and economies of countries in which you are operating e.g. levels of wealth. Exchange rates will vary, as will local taxes and tariffs. It may be also harder to chase creditors (credit risk).

Social – Cultural and demographic differences between countries which need to be adapted to market by market. Education and skill levels may differ also which may affect staffing.

Technical – Technological differences, particularly in developing nations.

Environmental – Countries with a different attitude and law in relation to environmental issues.

Legal – Each country has its own law and regulation which must be abided by in each new market entered.

Next we can consider the key strategic risks from Porter's 5 forces:

Customers – Will have different needs in each new market. They may have loyalty to existing products or brands.

Substitutes – There are likely to be different substitute products in each market. For example, a sport attempting to expand into new markets will likely come up against competition from other sports which are already popular in that country.

Suppliers – New relationships will need to be built with new suppliers. Supply may not be available in all new markets

Competitors – New local competition may be in each new market and will need to analysed and threats considered.

New Entrants – Are other competitors also entering that market? Will it become over-saturated?

Examples

Let's consider a European firm which sells high quality, branded handbags expanding into China, which has a growing market for designer handbags, as a specific example of how we might use these models to consider risk:

Political – Completely different political system – may impact the way regulations are set, and likely to be more bureaucratic than in Europe. Links with government

officials are key to success in China. Significant differences mean this is likely to be a high risk area.

Economic – The Chinese economy grew quickly throughout the start of the twenty first century suggesting a good country for growth and to target with growing middle classes. Changing exchange rates versus the local currency will be a risk that must be continually managed.

Social - The numbers of people now deemed middle class has increased dramatically which may offer opportunities for European products. European brands are seen as being of high quality and desirable. However, failing to ensure products also meet with local cultural norms is a key risk.

Technical - Technological differences is likely to be low risk for the market for handbags which does not depend on a particular technology.

Environmental - Environmental issues are generally seen as being of lower importance in China than the west, as the focus is more on growth than the environment. As such this is likely to be a low risk area.

Legal - China has a range of laws and restrictions that companies must abide by. There is a significant risk here, and being aware of these and ensuring all legal restrictions are met will be key to success.

Considering the key strategic risks from Porter's 5 forces:

Customers - There may be some new needs, and may have loyalty to existing products or brands; but Western brands for fashion products can be seen as positive. Care must be taken to understand customers and their needs and tailor products. There is medium risk in this area.

Customers could also be considered the outlets through which the company sells (e.g. department stores) and there is a significant risk that the major stores may not want to deal with this company.

Suppliers - In this case it is likely that no change in suppliers will be needed - the products are likely to be exported to China. As such this is a low risk area.

Competitors - There will be significant local competition and established brands. They may also attempt to resist a new entrant such as our company and as such this possibly the highest risk area of all.

New entrants - The company should also look at other brands that may be entering that market and ask what impact that may have on the success of the venture.

Substitutes - The local market may have other substitutes although it seems likely that handbags as a fashion item will be likely to grow for fashion conscious, wealthier consumers. Low risk.

7. Attitudes to risk

Risk appetite

Risk appetite looks at how much risk one is willing to accept. In organisations the level of risk appetite is often affected by attitudes of shareholders, directors and staff – often ingrained in the corporate culture.

Risk averse (wanting to avoid risk), **risk neutral** (balancing risk with reward) and **risk seeking** (happy to take risk if there are also possible high rewards) are examples of the terms that may be used to describe a risk appetite.

We often associate government organisations and long established companies with a risk-averse approach, while entrepreneurial organisations such as virgin are more risk seeking in nature. Listed companies often take a risk neutral approach as they have to balance risk management with taking new opportunities to get growth and higher profits for shareholders.

Risk tolerance

Risk tolerance is the level of deviation from the norm that will be accepted. The lower the risk tolerance, the lower the risks that can be undertaken and the greater the level of control that needs to be exerted to stay within the expected tolerance levels.

As you can see risk tolerance and risk appetite are two different ways of describing what is basically the same thing – a companies willingness, or otherwise, to take risks.

8. Human decision making and risk

Psychology and risk taking

Most decisions are made be people and therefore affected by people's beliefs, values, fears, desires and so on. A fear of taking risk is a key one for any manager, particularly if there are negative personal consequences. A manager may resist undertaking a new project if he fears there is only a small chance of it going wrong and him losing his job for example.

Up to the banking crisis of 2007 many bankers were accused of taking too many risks as doing this often resulted in large bonuses for them. There was also a culture of risk-taking, and so it seemed okay to take risks when everyone else was also taking them. When their investments turned sour this ended up being bad not just for some banks such as Lehman Brothers, but also many nations who propped the banks up to keep them profitable.

Link to governance

One of the aims of corporate governance is to prevent bias by individual directors or 'group think' (thinking alike) of boards of directors by implementation of measures such as scrutiny by independent non-executive directors, involvement in all directors in decision making and independent risk analysis.

CIMA P3 Course Notes

Chapter 2
Risk Management

1. Risk Management

Definition

Risk management is the identification, assessment, and prioritisation of risks followed by coordinated and economical application of resources to minimise, monitor, and control the probability and/or impact of unfortunate events or to maximise the realisation of opportunities.

A process to manage risks

In risk management, a prioritisation process is followed whereby the risks with the greatest loss (or impact) and the greatest probability of occurring are handled first, and risks with lower probability of occurrence and lower loss are handled in descending order.

In practice the process of assessing overall risk can be difficult, and balancing resources used to mitigate between risks with a high probability of occurrence but lower loss versus a risk with high loss but lower probability of occurrence can often be mishandled.

Balancing spending on risk management with benefits gained

Most risks can be minimised if enough money is spent on them, or extreme measures taken. Building sites can be made extremely safe with very strict procedures, the best staff training, safest equipment and a culture of safety being embedded in the organisation.

A key question though is just how much money and bureaucracy is invested in getting safer and safer, and where do you stop. There will come a point where so much money is spent on safety and the bureaucracy and controls are so stringent that the project is unprofitable and so is not viable.

Ideal risk management minimises spending on the management of risk while also minimising the negative effects of the risks themselves and achieving a fair balance between the two. What constitutes a fair balance is often a matter for the directors to decide and will often relate back to their risk appetite.

2. Principles of good risk management

ISO principles

The International Organisation for Standardisation (ISO) identifies the following principles of risk management:

Risk management should:

- **create value** – resources expended to mitigate risk should be less than the consequence of inaction, or put another way "the gain should exceed the pain"

- **be an integral part of organisational processes** (e.g. standard safety procedures)

- **be part of decision making** (e.g. when doing investment analysis, and part of the processes used in board meetings when making decisions)

- **explicitly address uncertainty and assumptions** (e.g. assumptions about future profits of a takeover target, and the likelihood of that materialising)

- **be systematic and structured** (e.g. safety procedures always followed no matter what)

- **be based on the best available information** (e.g. latest research on the safest methods of operation)

- **be tailorable** (and so flexible to different circumstances).

- **take into account human factors** (e.g. human error)

- **be transparent and inclusive** (so that all stakeholder needs are considered, so, for instance where higher risks are taken, shareholders will be informed)

- **be dynamic and responsive to change** (so as the organisation changes, so too are the controls to manage risk)

- **be capable of continual improvement and enhancement**

- **be continually or periodically re-assessed.**

Example

In the exam you can compare these principles to those used in the scenario to evaluate an organisation's risk management process, so for example, let's look at the following example:

Hunty Building had had an excellent safety record until the last 6 months since when there have been a number of on-site incidents, one in which 2 staff were severely injured. Six months ago the business took on a new project unlike any they had had before, which was authorised by the directors due to its extremely high profitability, but the time-scales were tight meaning the project was rushed and new staff brought in without the usual safety training. While the project was profitable, the organisation was criticised for the project and it has since lost a number of tenders for new projects as a result.

So, let's look through the principles of good risk management one by one and see which appear to have been adhered to and which have not - you might like to do your own review before reading on....

- **create value** - the project was profitable so value created although there were problems with tenders long term and so the project was not good value long term.

- **be an integral part of organisational processes** - no new processes seem to have been integrated into standard procedures to take account of the change in project type.

- **be part of decision making** - the project appears to have been accepted without the safety issues related to the new project type and the short deadline having been considered.

- **explicitly address uncertainty and assumptions** - uncertainties about the new project type appear to have been ignored.

- **be systematic and structured** - no new safety procedures seem to have been implemented based on the new project type

- **be based on the best available information** - no research undertaken into the safest methods of operation in this project type

- **be tailorable** - old procedures do not appear to have been tailored for the new project type

- **take into account human factors** - a lack of training was made available to new staff

- **be transparent and inclusive** - little information in the scenario on this point

- **be dynamic and responsive to change** - the key weakness was that controls were not changed for the new project type and lack of time

- **be capable of continual improvement and enhancement** - little information in the scenario on this point

- **be continually or periodically re-assessed** - no re-assessment undertaken of existing controls prior to this new project

3. Risk Management Process

There are a range of risk management approaches, which for the most part, consist of the following elements, performed, more or less, in the following order:

1) Identify threats

2) Assess the risk - the expected likelihood and consequences of specific types of threats on specific assets

3) Risk treatment - Identify ways to reduce or manage those risks

4) Implement risk management measures

5) Review and control

Step 1 - Identify threats

Risks are about events that, when triggered, cause problems. Hence, risk identification can **start with the source of problems**, or with the problem itself.

Examples of risk sources are:

- stakeholders of a project
- employees of a company
- the weather
- political change
- economic circumstances
- technological change
- competitors

Risks are related to identified threats. For example: the threat of losing money, the threat of abuse of confidential information or the threat of accidents and casualties. Threats can be related to sources therefore, so fore example if we take competitors we might say threats are: lower prices, new products or innovations, improved quality or service, better marketing, and so on.

Once a threat is identified, the **events that may be triggered can be investigated**. For example specific events related to competitors and lower prices might be: sales at particular times of the year, price reductions to sell off products that haven't sold well or responding to our price reductions.

The chosen method of identifying risks may depend on culture, industry practice and compliance. The identification methods are formed by templates or the development of templates for identifying source, problem or event. Common risk identification methods are:

www.astranti.com

Objectives-based risk identification

Organisations and project teams have objectives. Any event that may endanger achieving an objective partly or completely is identified as risk. An objective might be to make profits and so a competitor lowering prices would be a risk to those profits.

Scenario-based risk identification

In scenario analysis different scenarios are created. The scenarios may be the alternative ways to achieve an objective, or an analysis of the interaction of forces in, for example, a market or battle. Any event that triggers an undesired scenario alternative is identified as risk.

Taxonomy-based risk identification

Taxonomy-based risk identification is the use of a range of typical common risk categories to identify risks (e.g. Political risks, Economic risks, Financial risks - see chapter 1).

Common-risk checking

In several industries, lists with typical known risks are available. Each risk in the list can be checked for application to the organisation.

Risk charting

Risks are complied into a chart listing out:

- resources at risk
- threats to those resources
- modifying factors which may increase or decrease the risk
- consequences it is wished to avoid.

Identifying Risks Example

Throughout this section we'll use a simple example to demonstrate the process. Let's take a small jewellery shop in a local town centre and identify a few (of the many risks) they may face:

- Theft
- Economy declines reducing demand
- Cashflow weaknesses so they can't pay suppliers as debts fall due
- Legislation not adhered to (e.g. health and safety)
- Stock is purchased which can not be sold (or is sold at a loss)

- Errors in the accounting system

Step 2 – Assess the risks

Once risks have been identified, they must then be assessed as to their:

- potential severity of impact (generally a negative impact, such as damage or loss)
- the probability of occurrence.

These quantities can be either simple to measure, in the case of the value of a lost building, or impossible to know for sure in the case of the probability of an unlikely event occurring. Therefore, in the assessment process it is critical to make the best educated decisions in order to properly prioritize the implementation of the risk management plan.

These can then be plotted on a **risk map**.

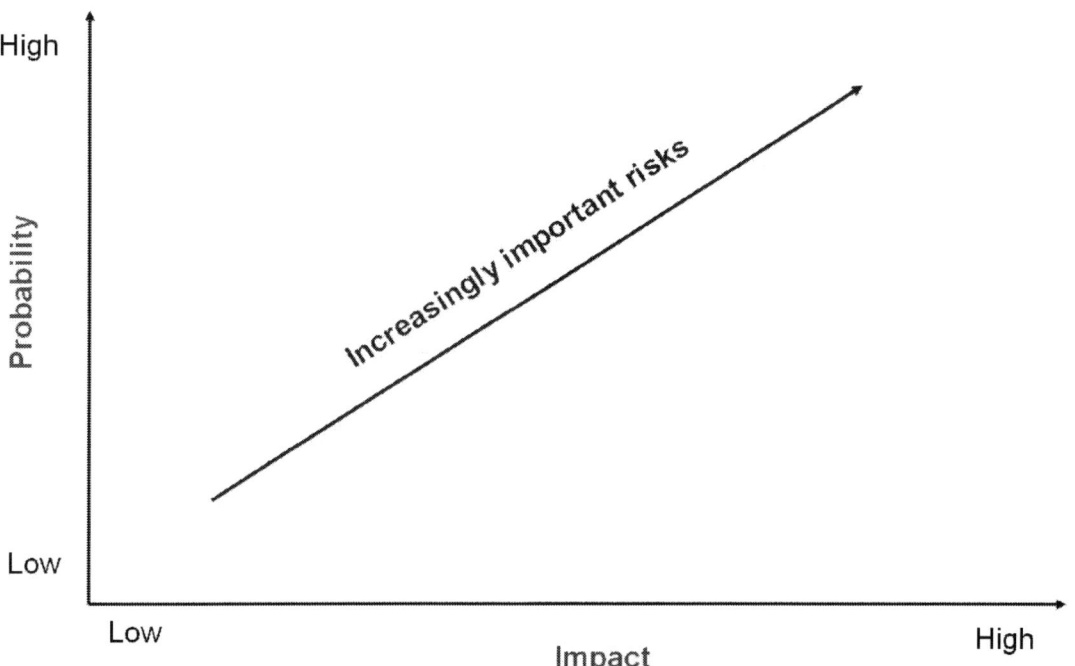

The risk map is a key method:

- of **analysing the risk** – the more important the risk, the more important it is that mitigating action is taken to reduce that risk

- of **reporting the risk** – e.g. reporting of risks by the audit or risk committee to the board or the board to the shareholders.

Example

So let's map out the risks in the Jewellery shop then:

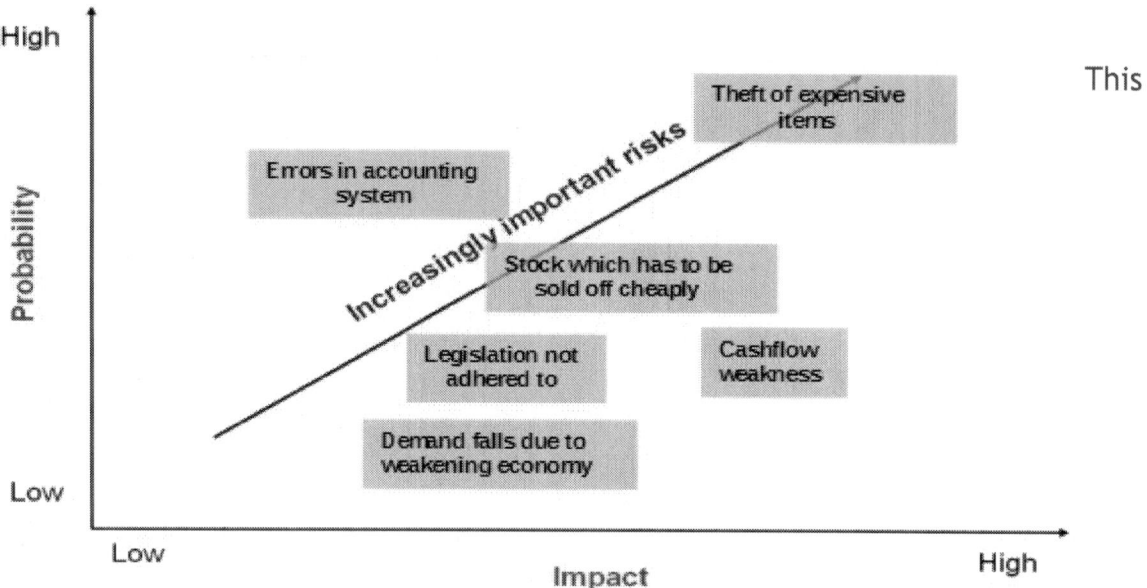

This highlights the real importance of our shop owner ensuring theft of expensive items is dealt with (high probability, high impact), while conversely that perhaps at the moment he doesn't need to worry about the changing economic circumstance (Low probability, medium to low impact). Although the impact of accounting errors is relatively low, the fact that it's quite likely suggests some greater control over the accounting process is needed.

Quantifying risk

Thus, there have been several theories and attempts to quantify risks. Numerous different risk formulae exist, but perhaps the most widely accepted formula for risk quantification is:

Composite Risk Index = Impact of Risk event x Probability of Occurrence

The impact of the risk event is commonly assessed on a scale of 1 to 5, where 1 and 5 represent the minimum and maximum possible impact of an occurrence of a risk (usually in terms of financial losses). However, the 1 to 5 scale can be arbitrary and need not be on a linear scale.

The probability of occurrence is likewise commonly assessed on a scale from 1 to 5, where 1 represents a very low probability of the risk event actually occurring while 5 represents a very high probability of occurrence.

The Composite Index thus can take values ranging (typically) from 1 through 25, and this range is usually arbitrarily divided into three sub-ranges. The overall risk assessment is then Low, Medium or High, depending on the sub-range containing the calculated value of the Composite Index. For instance, the three sub-ranges could be defined as 1 to 8, 9 to 16 and 17 to 25.

Financial quantification of risk

The same formula can also be used to predict the financial impact of a risk, so if the probability of fire happening at head-office happening is 25% and the impact would be £100,000 then the expected value of 25% x £100,000 of £25,000 can be a useful figure. This would, for instance, be the maximum worth spending on insurance each year.

Difficulties in assessment

The fundamental difficulty in risk quantification is determining the probability (or rate) of occurrence since statistical information is not available on all kinds of past incidents. Is there really a 25% chance of a fire occurring – how accurate is that really?

Furthermore, evaluating the severity of the consequences (impact) is often quite difficult. How much damage would the fire actually cause – it could be small or large.

Nevertheless, risk assessment should produce such information for the management of the organisation that the primary risks are easy to understand and that the risk management decisions may be prioritised.

Step 3 – Risk Treatment/Management

Once risks have been identified and assessed, techniques to manage the risk fall into one or more of the four major (TARA) categories:

Transfer   - Sharing with another party e.g. Outsource or insure

Avoidance   - Eliminate, withdraw from or not become involved

Reduction   - Control and mitigate

Accept   - Accept the risk and budget for its possible occurrence

Risk transfer

Defined as "sharing with another party the burden of loss or the benefit of gain, from a risk, and the measures to reduce a risk."

This is usually done on one of two ways:

1. Insuring the risk and hence passing the 'financial risk' on to the insurance company. The risk of a ring being stolen is a good one to pass onto an insurer for instance.

2. Outsourcing – so that the risk is passed to the outsourcer as part of the contract. If, for example if the jewellery shop was having an extension it might be good to get an agreed price for the completed work, so that any unforeseen issues are passed onto the builder and not the shop owner.

Note that some element of the risk is often retained by the company. In the event of a fire, the business may be able to reclaim the financial losses, but there may be reputational risk, the negative impact of staff caught up in the fire, or a loss of key information that is difficult to reproduce.

Risk avoidance

This typically involves not performing an activity that could carry risk.

Our jeweller might, for instance, never stock items worth more than £10,000 to completely avoid the risk associated with holding such high value items.

On the downside, avoiding risks also means losing out on the potential gain that accepting (retaining) the risk may have allowed – selling those higher value items for instance. Another example would be to not entering into a new business opportunity; it avoids the risk, but also stops the possibility of earning more profits.

Risk reduction

Risk reduction involves reducing the severity of the loss or the likelihood of the loss from occurring. For example, sprinklers are designed to put out a fire to reduce the risk of loss by fire, while locks on doors reduce the risk of theft, as do security guards.

Our jeweller might put controls in place to reduce the risk of accounting errors highlighted earlier. This could include:

- checking the balance sheet balances
- using control accounts
- balancing the bank reconciliation
- input checks
- shop owner review of bookkeepers work
- using a reputed book-keeper or accounting firm.

Risk retention/acceptance

Retention involves accepting the loss, or benefit of gain, from a risk when it occurs. True self insurance falls in this category. Risk retention is a viable strategy for small risks where the cost of insuring against the risk would be greater over time than the total losses sustained. All risks that are not avoided or transferred are retained by default. This includes risks that are so large or catastrophic that they either cannot be insured against or the premiums would be infeasible.

Our jeweller might, for instance, accept small thefts, and not bother insuring for those which in total are valued at less than £100. He might also accept that

occasionally staff will be ill and that will be out of his control and he'll just have to work harder that day to cover them being away.

Any amounts of potential loss (risk) over the amount insured is **retained risk**. This may also be acceptable if the chance of a very large loss is small or if the cost to insure for greater coverage amounts is so great it would hinder the goals of the organisation too much.

Create a risk management/treatment plan

For each risk identified, appropriate controls or countermeasures should be selected. For example, an observed high risk of computer viruses could be mitigated by acquiring and implementing anti virus software. A good risk management plan should contain a schedule for control implementation and responsible persons for those actions.

Each approach must be approved by the appropriate level of management. For instance, a risk concerning the image of the organisation should have top management decision behind it whereas IT management would have the authority to decide on computer virus risks.

The risks and agreed methods of managing these risks are summarised in a **Risk Management/Treatment Plan**, which documents the decisions about how each of the identified risks should be handled.

Step 4 - Implementation

Implementation follows all of the planned methods for mitigating the effect of the risks. It simply means taking the action agreed.

Example

Our jeweller will now need to action his risk management plan. This might, for example, include:

- purchasing insurance policies for the risks that have been decided to be transferred to an insurer
- taking security measures to prevent theft
- and not stocking items deemed to be too high risk
- changing his book-keeper to someone more reliable

Step 5 - Review and control

Initial risk management plans will never be perfect. Practice, experience, and actual loss results will necessitate changes in the plan and contribute information to allow different decisions to be made in dealing with the risks being faced.

Risk analysis results and management plans should be updated periodically.

There are two primary reasons for this:

- to evaluate whether the previously selected controls are still applicable and effective
- to evaluate the possible risk level changes in the business environment. Changes in procedures, technology, schedules, budgets, market conditions, political environment, or other factors typically require re-assessment of risks.

Example

Again, let's take our jeweller; one risk identified was the loss of demand due to the economy worsening. During boom times that might be deemed very low likelihood and not worth considering, but if a recession hit, it would become more likely (and move to the right in our risk map). We would also be in a better position to assess the exact impact, which may be higher than initially expected.

An increase in thefts in other stores locally might also highlight the need for greater security.

The world is a continually changing place and so our risks need to be continuously re-evaluated.

4. Gross vs Net Risks

One of the issues we have when examining risks is whether to look at gross risks or net risks.

For the moment let's say that our jeweller has a number of items in our store. One is a £10,000 diamond ring which is fully insured and the other a £50 pair of earrings which is of too low a value to be part of our insurance policy.

Gross risk is the risk before any mitigating action, such as insurance. It is useful as it shows us the full extent of any risk we are taking to ensure that mitigating actions are taken; and indeed in this case our jeweller has been sensible and insured the diamond ring. He might also be sensible to ensure that ring is kept locked up in a safe when it's not out on display.

Net risk is the risk after all risk management measures and controls have been taken into account. Here, our ring is fully insured, while the earrings are not. Our net risk is actually higher for the earrings than the ring. In fact, perhaps it's the earrings that should be being locked up not the diamond ring!

Now this example simplifies things, because it of course ignores other factors like the likelihood of the rings and earring being stolen, the distress that a theft would have on our shop owner, and the hassle of completing insurance forms. However it does demonstrate nicely the key issues in relation to gross and net risks.

Often **risk managers** will be **most focused on net risk**, as this tell them about the amount of risk left unmanaged and helps them decide whether that is acceptable (our 'accept' strategy under TARA) or whether more controls are needed (our 'reduce' strategy under TARA).

Internal auditors take a different approach, when they do their reviews. They tend to focus on **gross risks**, as they ask the question 'Are our biggest risks fully controlled?". They are concerned with the controls that are in place and whether those controls are working, and this must be noted for risk managers also – it's all very well thinking you have good controls, but if they are over-ridden in some way the risk is again the gross risk.

Our jewellery shop owner may have a good insurance policy, but then forget to renew it and suddenly be exposed to the full risk of theft of that expensive ring. Jerome Kerviel lost €5bn at Societe Generale in 2008 – the net risks for the bank seemed low due to the significant controls in place over excessive trading by traders such as Mr Kerviel, but as soon as those controls were over-ridden by him the full extent of the gross risk was revealed and, unfortunately for the bank, a huge loss incurred.

5. Enterprise risk management (ERM) - COSO

Definition

Enterprise risk management (ERM) is a risk-based approach to managing an enterprise, and is one of the world's most common methodologies used to manage risk in an organisation. It aims to help organisations understand the risks facing them and develop control strategies to ensure they are effectively managed. It was developed in 2004 by COSO (the Committee of Sponsoring Organisations of the Treadway Commission).

It is basically a formal, standard, structured approach to the methodology outlined in the previous section....

The ERM Cube

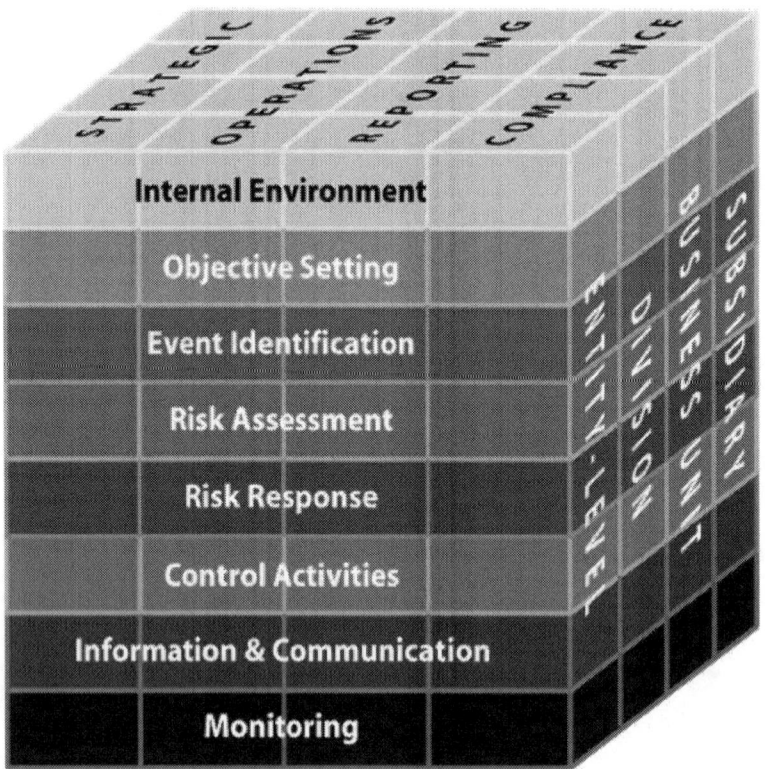

The ERM cube represents how ERM works throughout the organisation. The four ERM objectives are shown on the top of the cube. The eight 'processes' which you have to go through to undertake ERM are shown on the front face, while the elements on the right face aim to show that these should be followed in every part of the organisation i.e. in each subsidiary, business unit, division and indeed the organisation as a whole.

Objectives of enterprise risk management

The enterprise risk management framework is geared to achieving the following four key objectives:

- Strategic: high-level strategic goals, aligned with and supporting its mission
- Operations: effective and efficient use of its resources at an operational level in the business
- Reporting: reliability of reporting (e.g. financial reports)
- Compliance: compliance with applicable laws and regulations

Eight framework components

The eight framework components match very closely to the standard risk management approach outlined earlier – as you review these you will notice distinct similarities, as any good risk management model will tend to follow the same basic structure.

The eight components of enterprise risk management are:

Internal environment: The internal environment encompasses the tone of an organisation, and sets the basis for how risk is viewed and addressed by an entity's people, including risk management philosophy and risk appetite, integrity and ethical values, and the environment in which they operate. This is also often called the 'control environment'.

The stronger the internal environment the less likely risks will materialise. For example, if managers always review risks inherent in each key decision and are encouraged to manage any risks found, then the likelihood of there being risk issues in an organisation is lower. In banking before the 2007/08 crisis, risk taking was the culture, and in this environment there was always a higher risk that problems would occur.

Objective setting: Objectives must exist before management can identify potential events affecting their achievement. Enterprise risk management ensures that management has in place a process to set objectives and that the chosen objectives support and align with the entity's mission and are consistent with its risk appetite.

ERM notes that the main risks are those that prevent the organisations goals from being achieved. If the main basis of success of a company, and a key goal therefore, is good customer service than risks that would prevent that happening will be key to identify and manage.

Event identification: Internal and external events affecting achievement of an entity's objectives must be identified. What are the actual times when poor service

may result, for instance. Perhaps it would be due to being out of stock of items people want to buy, or due to poorly trained staff.

ERM distinguishes between risks and opportunities. While risks are considering things that could go wrong, and so managed by the remainder of the risk management process, opportunities are ideas that can move the organisation forward towards its goals, and are channelled back to management for review and implementation.

Risk assessment: Risks are analysed, considering likelihood and impact, as a basis for determining how they should be managed. They are mapped out onto a risk map and are assessed on a both a gross and net risk basis.

Risk response: Management selects risk responses – avoiding, accepting, reducing, or transferring risk – developing a set of actions to align risks with the entity's risk tolerances and risk appetite.

Control activities: Policies and procedures are established and implemented to help ensure the risk responses are effectively carried out.

Information and communication: Relevant information is identified, captured, and communicated in a form and time frame that enable people to carry out their responsibilities. Effective communication also occurs in a broader sense, flowing down, across, and up the entity.

Monitoring: The entirety of enterprise risk management is monitored and modifications made as necessary. Monitoring is accomplished through ongoing management activities (e.g. managers reviewing controls or regular reports to the board) and separate evaluations, such as a review by the internal auditors.

6. CIMA's Risk Management Cycle

The CIMA risk management cycle is another risk management model, similar in nature to the COSO model of risk management. It outlines the following steps for risk management:

1. Establish a risk management group and set goals.

2. Identify risk areas.

3. Understand and assess the scale of risk.

4. Develop a risk response strategy.

5. Implement the strategy and allocate responsibilities.

6. Implement and monitor the suggested controls.

7. Review and refine the process and do it again.

You'll notice that this is simply another variation of the generic steps at the start of this chapter – the 5 steps there simply having been split out into 7 for this model.

Unlike the COSO model, CIMA's risk management cycle is not specifically mentioned in the syllabus.

7. Problems of risk management

Managing and organisations risks effectively can be a difficult process. Here are some of the key reasons:

Subjective

Probability and impact can often be subjective, making the degree of risk hard to assess. The best approach to managing the risk is also often subjective.

Bureaucracy

Prioritising the risk management processes too highly can make the organisation or project **overly bureaucratic** with every processes requiring detailed controls. It can also mean that some projects never get started or are delayed, as the risks are assessed or are perceived as unknown or excessively high.

Stifle innovation

The bureaucracy and a risk averse approach may also result in a **lack of innovation and losing competitive edge** to faster moving competitors. Risky projects may simply be avoided where small, flexible, unbureaucratic organisations may simply "go for it". While the risk of failure is avoided the competitor who took the risk and was successful may now get a competitive edge.

Expensive and resource intensive

Spending too much time assessing and managing unlikely risks can also divert resources that could be used more profitably elsewhere. There are also costs associated both with the risk management process (e.g. risk committee and risk manager salaries) and the controls that are put in place to manage risk (e.g. costs of insurance or security measures).

Human error

Human failures such as simple errors or mistakes can lead to inadequate responses to risk.

Controls can be circumvented

Controls can be circumvented by collusion of two or more people or by an IT literate employee, and management has the ability to override risk management decisions. People are often motivated by personal gain and not managing risk, and so may circumvent controls for those reasons. E.g. Jerome Kerviel at Societe Generale lost €5bn through circumventing the banks controls over trading.

8. Assurance mapping

Stakeholders such as banks, shareholders and suppliers need **assurance** that the business is meeting their needs. The bank will want 'assurance' that their debts will be repaid; the investor that the business is performing well and will continue to do so in the future, and the employee that they will have a job! One major part of assurance is the provision of reliable financial information in the financial statements. Another, and our key focus here, is assurance that the organisation's key risks are well managed.

An **assurance map** is a documented plan of all assurance needed and how that is met and outlines:

- the people to whom assurance should be provided (e.g. shareholders, banks etc.)

- the nature of the assurance - what do they want to be 'assured' about e.g. that the company is a going concern, or that their loan will be repaid

- how the assurance will be provided (e.g. through financial statements or risk management and control)

- how the board of directors will ensure that information provided to them is correct and truthful (e.g. through internal audit reviews)

- the risk management culture (the general way everyone in the organisation approaches risk) and how that is monitored and reviewed.

- An outline of all the key risks and how assurance is provided against all those risks to ensure there are no potential gaps. For our jewellers that could look like this:

Key Risk	Control 1	Control 2	Control 3	Control 4
£10,000 diamond ring is stolen	Locked in safe whenever not on display	Insurance	Shop-keeper always in store when ring is on display	Unbreakable glass in windows to prevent theft when on display
Economy declines reducing demand	Shop leased on low rent to keep fixed costs low	Excess stock kept to a minimum	Monitor changing economic circumstances	Annual strategic review
Cash flow weakness means suppliers can not be paid	Bank balances monitored weekly	Monthly cashflow forecasts prepared	Overdraft arrangements with bank	Good relationship with suppliers maintained to gain flexibility when needed

Ideally an assurance map should be updated regularly, and at least annually, to reflect changing risks.

9. Risk register

A risk register is a risk management tool commonly used as a central repository for all risks identified by the organisation. This ensures that all risks once identified are recorded, along with the mitigating actions which have been decided upon. The risk register should be regularly updated to ensure it is kept up to date.

Typically a risk register contains:

- A description of the risk
- The impact should this event actually occur
- The probability of its occurrence
- Risk Score (the multiplication of Probability and Impact)
- A summary of the planned response should the event occur
- A summary of the mitigation (the actions taken in advance to reduce the probability and/or impact of the event)

The risks are often ranked by Risk Score so as to highlight the highest priority risks to all involved.

CIMA P3 Course Notes

Chapter 3
Governance and Reporting

1. Governance

Definition

Corporate governance is the way organisations are directed, administered and controlled, with the aim of ensuring that the organisation is run in a way that is right for all stakeholders, in particular the shareholders.

Corporate governance therefore includes managing the relationships among the many players involved (the stakeholders) and managing the organisation's goals and strategies. The principal players include the shareholders, management, and the board of directors. Other stakeholders include employees, suppliers, customers, banks and other lenders, regulators, the environment and the community at large.

The agency problem

One key element of governance is the management of the varying needs of different stakeholders.

One particular conflict which can commonly arise is the **agency problem**. The shareholders (the principal) employ the directors (the agent) to run the business on their behalf. Although the directors should be running the business in the shareholders interests (they have a fiduciary duty to do so), it is inevitable that their own personal interests will be considered too, for instance when it comes to salaries paid. This conflict is the agency problem.

One issue with the agency problem is **information asymmetry**. The directors have more information about the company than the shareholders, and as a result the shareholders are not always able to fully hold directors accountable for decisions made. Governance regulation often aims to overcome the agency problem, by finding ways of reducing bias of directors and improving accountability and disclosure of information.

The need for governance

In recent years there has been significant interest in the corporate governance practices of modern corporations, particularly in relation to accountability, since the high-profile collapses of a number of large corporations.

In the UK the Cadbury report was produced in 1992 after the collapses of BCCI, the Mirror Group and Polly Peck, whilst in the U.S., there was increasing focus from 2001 after scandals including Enron and WorldCom. Their demise was quickly followed by the U.S. government passing the Sarbanes-Oxley Act (2002) which imposed strict governance standards in US companies.
Comparable failures in Australia (HIH, One.Tel) are associated with the eventual passage of the CLERP 9 reforms. Similar corporate failures in other countries stimulated increased regulatory interest (e.g. Parmalat in Italy).

2. Principles of corporate governance

Contemporary discussions of corporate governance tend to refer to principles raised in three documents released since 1990: The Cadbury Report (UK, 1992), the Principles of Corporate Governance (OECD, 1998 and 2004), the Sarbanes-Oxley Act of 2002 (US, 2002).

The Cadbury and OECD reports present general principals around which businesses are expected to operate to assure proper governance. The Sarbanes-Oxley Act, informally referred to as Sarbox or Sox, is an attempt by the federal government in the United States to legislate several of the principles recommended in the Cadbury and OECD reports.

The key principles are as follows.

Rights and equitable treatment of shareholders

Organisations should respect the rights of shareholders and help shareholders to exercise those rights. They can help shareholders exercise their rights by openly and effectively communicating information and by encouraging shareholders to participate in general meetings.

Interests of other stakeholders

Organisations should recognise that they have legal, contractual, social, and market driven obligations to non-shareholder stakeholders, including employees, investors, creditors, suppliers, local communities, customers, and policy makers.

Role and responsibilities of the board

The board needs sufficient, relevant skills and understanding to review and challenge management performance. It also needs adequate size so there are a wide range of people contributing decisions with a wide range of knowledge and experience.

There should be independence and objectivity in decisions. This may be achieved through the use of independent non-executive directors.

Integrity and ethical behaviour

Integrity should be a fundamental requirement in choosing corporate officers and board members. Organisations should develop a code of conduct for their directors and executives that promotes ethical and responsible decision making.

Disclosure and transparency

Organisations should be open and transparent in their dealings, particularly with shareholders. The should disclose key financial information in the financial statements as well as any other relevant information, such as major decisions made, director's salaries, key risks or problems and the strategic direction of the business.

3. The UK Code of Corporate Governance

Applies to UK Listed companies

The UK Corporate Governance Code 2010 is a set of principles of good corporate governance aimed at companies **listed on the London Stock Exchange**.

Public listed companies are required to disclose how they have complied with the code, and explain where they have not applied the code - in what the code refers to as 'comply or explain'

Note that this means that there is no legal obligation to actually follow the rules of the code, with the aim of providing the Directors with the flexibility to diverge from the code where they feel it is in stakeholders' best interests. Full disclosure where they did not comply and the reasons for this should enable shareholders to raise objections if they do not agree.

In defiance of combined code rules, Stuart Rose, became the Executive Chairman (i.e. both Chairman and CEO) of Marks and Spencer in 2008 as the directors believed it was best for the company. Following significant shareholder protests and negative media coverage he stepped down from this role in 2010.

Private companies are also encouraged to conform; however there is no requirement for disclosure of compliance in private company accounts.

A principles based approach

The Code adopts a **principles-based approach** in the sense that it provides general guidelines of best practice. This contrasts with a **rules-based approach** which rigidly defines exact provisions that must be adhered to, as with the US Sarbanes Oxley legislation.

Contents of the UK combined code

Section A: Leadership

Every company should be headed by an **effective board** which is collectively responsible for the long-term success of the company. Decisions should be taken by the board as a whole with all directors contributing to the decision making process.

There should be a clear **division of responsibilities at the head of the company** between the running of the board (Chairman) and the executive responsibility for the running of the company's business (CEO). No one individual should have unfettered powers of decision making.

The **chairman** is responsible for leadership of the board and ensuring its effectiveness on all aspects of its role.

There should be independent **non-executive directors (NEDs)** who should constructively challenge and help develop proposals on strategy. They bring independence to decision making, and provide their expertise to support making a good decision. They also sit on committees, such as the remuneration, audit and nomination committees, that need an element of independence to them.

Section B: Effectiveness

The board and its committees should have the appropriate **balance of skills, experience, independence and knowledge of the company** to enable them to discharge their respective duties and responsibilities effectively.

There should be a formal, rigorous and transparent procedure for the

appointment of new directors to the board. This will typically involve the use of a **Nomination committee** which includes independent Non-Executive directors, to ensure a fair, unbiased process is followed.

All directors should be able to **allocate sufficient time** to the company to discharge their responsibilities effectively.

All directors should receive **induction** on joining the board and should regularly **update** and refresh their skills and knowledge.

The board should be supplied in a timely manner with **information** in a form and of a quality appropriate to enable it to discharge its duties.

The board should undertake a formal and rigorous annual evaluation of its own performance and that of its committees and individual directors.

All directors should be **submitted for re-election** at regular intervals, subject to continued satisfactory performance.

Section C: Accountability

The board should **disclose** a balanced and understandable assessment of the company's position and prospects, in the financial statements.

The board is responsible for determining the nature and extent of the significant risks it is willing to take in achieving its strategic objectives. The board should maintain **sound risk management and internal control systems**.

The board should establish formal and transparent arrangements for considering how they should apply the corporate reporting and risk management and internal control principles and for maintaining an appropriate relationship with the **company's auditor.**

The **role of the the audit committee** is to control and manage the 3 elements in this section (financial statements, risk and control and relationship with the auditor).

Section D: Remuneration

Levels of remuneration should be sufficient to attract, retain and motivate directors of the quality required to run the company successfully, but a company should avoid paying more than is necessary for this purpose. A significant proportion of executive directors' remuneration should be structured so as to link rewards to corporate and individual performance.(With an increasing emphasis on long term performance)

There should be a formal and transparent procedure for developing **policy** on executive remuneration and for fixing the remuneration packages of individual directors. No director should be involved in deciding his or her own remuneration.

To be independent most organisations have a separate **nomination committee** staffed by NEDs who are responsible for implementation of this section of the combined code.

Section E: Relations with Shareholders

There should be a **dialogue with shareholders** based on the mutual understanding of objectives. The board as a whole has responsibility for ensuring that a satisfactory dialogue with shareholders takes place.

The board should use the **Annual General Meeting (AGM)** to communicate with investors and to encourage their participation.

The code most commonly used in the exam

As a good, general set of principles it is also the one you should **most commonly use in the exam** irrelevant of which country or type of organisation the question is set. Use it as an example of good principles even if that organisation is not obligated to use it. It's a bit dull, but it's one of the key things you must learn for this exam!

4. Committees responsible for risk management

Risk management at board level is the responsibility of the board as a whole. They usually delegate that responsibility to one of two committees. Let's look a the role of these committees.

Audit committee

The combined code specifically sets out clear responsibilities for the audit committee as follows:

- monitoring the integrity of the **financial statements** and any formal announcements relating to financial performance.

- reviewing **internal financial controls** and, unless there is a separate board risk committee, reviewing the company's **internal control and risk management systems**.

- monitoring and reviewing the effectiveness of the **internal audit function**.

- making recommendations to the board in relation to the **appointment, re-appointment and removal of the external auditor** and approve the remuneration and terms of engagement of the auditor.

- reviewing the **auditor's independence** and objectivity.

- developing and implementing the **non-audit services policy** (with the aim that auditor independence is not compromised by significant non-audit fees).

The audit committee should be staffed by independent Non-Executive Directors to bring independence to this key oversight role.

Risk committee

Although not a requisite of the UK's code of corporate governance it is also worth noting that many organisations also have a **risk committee** who's role is to assist the Board of Directors in fulfilling its oversight responsibilities with regard to the risk management and control of the organisation.

If there is no risk committee this role will be undertaken by the Audit Committee. Whereas an audit committee should consist of NEDs, the risk committee often includes executive directors, with the aim of using their business expertise and knowledge to identify and fully control the risks of the organisation. A risk committee tends to be deemed necessary in organisations where risks are high, specialist knowledge is needed and significant time is required (more than can be given by the Audit committee and their 'part time' NEDs). Banks are an example of organisations who have risk committees for exactly this reason.

5. Director's pay and governance

Remuneration and governance

One key governance risk which is a key problem in agency theory is that directors are responsible for their own pay, and as such are biased towards high pay awards, which is contradictory to the needs of shareholders – the higher the pay the lower the profits.....

However, high pay can be justified if it serves to:

- attract high quality staff
- retain those staff
- motivate them to work hard and increase profits.

Basic pay and benefits (pensions, company and car) should therefore be comparable to similar organisations or otherwise the best candidates will go elsewhere, but not excessive.

Ideally a significant proportion of executive directors' remuneration should be structured so as to link rewards to corporate and individual performance.

This could be through:

- Performance related pay (e.g. related to increased revenues or profits)
- Executive share options – the option to purchase shares in the future at a set price. Directors will be motived to increase the share price to above the set price, which will reward both themselves and the shareholders.
- Bonuses – ideally based on achieving performance targets

The role of the nomination committee

To ensure greater independence in director's remuneration, most organisations have a separate **nomination committee** staffed by NEDs who are responsible for:

- developing a formal and transparent procedure for developing **policy** on executive remuneration
- fixing the remuneration packages of individual directors.

6. Key governance risks

The key risks of poor governance are as follows:

Lack of wider business knowledge and diversity in decision making

Overcome by:

- The use of independent NEDs with a wide range of expertise from a variety of backgrounds.

- A wide range of executive directors on the board bringing knowledge of different parts of the business to board discussions.

- All directors being present at board meetings and contributing to the debate and decision making process

- Directors given relevant training in all aspects of the business, including an induction when they join.

Too much power to one person at the top of the organisation

Overcome by:

- splitting the CEO and Chairman role so that no-one person has complete control of the organisation – the Chairman controls the board and relations with shareholders, and the CEO the day to day running of the business.

- All directors being present at board meetings and contributing to the debate and decision making process

Lack of communication and transparency with shareholders

Overcome by:

- Clear responsibility given to the Chairman for this role

- Regular meetings with shareholders where strategic issues are openly discussed

- Annual financial statements prepared using current financial accounting regulations, audited by an independent auditor and overseen by the audit committee of independent Non-executive Directors.

- A range of other relevant information disclosed in the financial statements e.g. directors salary, review of performance etc.

Directors vote themselves too high a remuneration unrelated to their performance

Overcome by:

- Remuneration being decided by a remuneration committee of independent Non-Executive Directors.

- Pay being directly liked to performance

Bias in the recruitment process

Overcome by:

- Board recruitment being decided by a nomination committee which includes a significant representation of independent Non-Executive Directors.

- Fair, objective assessment criteria being applied to applications.

Poor risk management and control

Overcome by:

- Board responsibility for risk and control, with responsibility usually allocated to the audit committee (or risk committee if one is present).

- Regular review of risks and controls at board level, and as part of disclosure in financial statements

- Use of internal auditors, who independently review controls against risks, and report key control weaknesses to the Audit Committee.

7. Risk Reporting

Reporting risk in the financial statements

At the heart of the principles of corporate governance is the idea of transparency. As part of this the directors should clearly disclose with shareholders the key risks in the business.

In the UK the formally required reporting of risk in financial statements under the 2012 Combined Code is actually minimal. The UK's code of corporate governance states:

*"The board should, at least annually, conduct a review of the effectiveness of the company's risk management and internal control systems and **should report to shareholders that they have done so**. The review should cover all material controls, including financial, operational and compliance controls."*

However many companies choose to disclose much more information about key risks than this minimum requirement, and many include a statement of key risks and how those risks are being managed, similar in many ways to the "Assurance Mapping" approached discussed in the risk management section. Here is a sample of an assurance map for a jewellery shop:

Key Risk	Control 1	Control 2	Control 3	Control 4
£10,000 diamond ring is stolen	Locked in safe whenever not on display	Insurance	Shop-keeper always in store when ring is on display	Unbreakable glass in windows to prevent theft when on display
Economy declines reducing demand	Shop leased on low rent to keep fixed costs low	Excess stock kept to a minimum	Monitor changing economic circumstances	Annual strategic review
Cash flow weakness means suppliers can not be paid	Bank balances monitored weekly	Monthly cashflow forecasts prepared	Overdraft arrangements with bank	Good relationship with suppliers maintained to gain flexibility when needed

The balance must always be made between being open and transparent, and protecting the businesses needs. Too much openness about some risks could result in some users of the accounts misinterpreting the situation, or in the disclosure of sensitive business critical information, and so the directors need to aim for balance.

Shareholder meetings and responses

The combined code does encourage regular meetings with the shareholders, including active use of the Annual General Meeting, and it is vital that information on the business, its strategy, performance and risks are discussed there, and that shareholder views and listened to, discussed by the board and taken into account in the decision making process.

CIMA P3 Course Notes

Chapter 4
Internal Control

1. Internal Control

What is internal control?

Internal control is a process designed to help the organisation accomplish specific goals or objectives. This aim is to control what the organisation does and how it does it within the bounds of the organisation's aims.

Examples include:

- Standardised procedures to ensure activities are done in a consistent way
- Reviews and checks for quality and accuracy
- Performance measurement and review
- Detailed strategic and operational plans – to guide and control people and processes towards key aims
- Authorisation checks on transactions
- Security around key assets
- HR controls such as training, recruitment checks, time sheets, supervision etc.

Internal control can often be seen as either moving the organisation towards goals (e.g. the strategic plans) or stopping "bad things happening" e.g. fraud, errors, theft (e.g. security controls).

Under the **COSO** Internal Control-Integrated Framework, internal control is broadly defined as:

"a process, effected by an entity's board of directors, management, and other personnel, designed to provide reasonable assurance regarding the achievement of objectives in the following categories:

a) Effectiveness and efficiency of operations;

b) Reliability of financial reporting; and

c) Compliance with laws and regulations."

What are internal control systems and what is their purpose?

An internal control system is the system of controls applied to the organisation as a whole to help to prevent organisational risks.

According to the UK's Turnbull report (which later formed part of the Combined code) "An internal control system encompasses the policies, processes, tasks, behaviours and other aspects of a company that, taken together have the following **purpose**:

- facilitate its **effective and efficient operation** by enabling it to respond appropriately to significant business, operational, financial, compliance and other risks **to achieve the company's objectives.** This includes the **safeguarding of assets** from inappropriate use or from loss and fraud, and ensuring that liabilities are identified and managed;

- help ensure the **quality of internal and external reporting**. This requires the maintenance of proper records and processes that generate a flow of timely, relevant and reliable information from within and outside the organisation; help ensure **compliance with applicable laws and regulations**, **and** also **internal policies** with respect to the conduct of business.

Notice the broad similarity between the key elements of the COSO definition and the Turnbull definition.

2. Key features of internal control systems

COSO defines internal control systems as having five key components:

Control Environment

Sets the tone for the organisation, influencing the control consciousness of its people. It reflects the culture in the organisation. For example, where there is a culture where staff always abiding by standard procedures, then the control environment is stronger than somewhere where they are often ignored. If there is a culture of 'quality in all we do' as in a TQM environment, then there are likely to be fewer errors and quality problems, than somewhere where quality is not a cultural focus. The control environment is the foundation for all other components of internal control.

Ultimately the organisation should aim to **embed risk management and control** as a part of a culture within the organisation. It should be a natural part of the way everyone operates.

Risk Assessment

The identification and analysis of relevant risks to the achievement of objectives, forming a basis for how the risks should be managed.

Information and Communication

Systems or processes that support the identification, capture, and exchange of information in a form and time frame that enable people to carry out their responsibilities. Management accounting information is a good example of relevant control information that must be communicated to the relevant staff to act on.

Control Activities

The policies and procedures that help ensure management directives are carried out. E.g. Security, authorisation, accounting controls, supervision etc.

Monitoring

Processes should be used to assess the quality of internal control performance over time, so controls are reviewed and updated to ensure key risks continue to be well managed. This ensures that the organisation is **responsive to evolving risks.**

Part of the monitoring process is ensuring **timely reporting to management** so that they can monitor the controls effectively and take any necessary action if they are not working effectively.

3. Role of key stakeholders in control

Pervasive nature of internal control

According to the COSO Framework, **everyone in an organisation** has responsibility for internal control to some extent. Virtually all employees produce information used in the internal control system or take other actions needed to affect control. This is often described at the: **pervasive nature of internal control**. All personnel should be responsible for communicating upward problems in operations, non-compliance with codes of conduct, or other policy violations or illegal actions.

It is therefore vital that all employees have **training in risk management and control**, ideally as it relates to their department and their role. Organising this training is usually the responsibility of the risk manager (see below).

Key stakeholders in the control process

In addition there are a range of specific stakeholders who have a major role to play in organisational control:

Management

The Chief Executive Officer (the top manager) of the organisation has overall responsibility for designing and implementing effective internal control. More than any other individual, the chief executive sets the "tone at the top" that affects integrity and ethics and other factors of a positive control environment.

In a large company, the chief executive fulfils this duty by providing leadership and direction to senior managers and reviewing the way they're controlling the business.

Senior managers, in turn, assign responsibility for establishment of more specific internal control policies and procedures to personnel responsible for the unit's functions.

Board of Directors

Management is accountable to the board of directors, which provides governance, guidance and oversight. Effective board members are objective, capable and inquisitive. They also have a knowledge of the entity's activities and environment, and commit the time necessary to fulfil their board responsibilities.

A strong, active board, particularly when coupled with effective upward communications channels and capable financial, legal and internal audit functions, is often best able to identify and correct control weaknesses.

Audit committee

The audit committee oversee the work of the internal and external auditors, and are often responsible for risk and control on behalf of the board of directors. They are usually staffed by non-executive directors so they are independent of the day to day running of the business.

Internal Auditors

The internal auditors of the organisation also measure the effectiveness of internal control through their efforts. They assess whether the controls are properly designed, implemented and working effectively, and make recommendations on how to improve internal control.

External auditors

External auditors will review controls that relate to the production and accuracy of the financial statements. The better the controls the less detailed testing they need to do in their work. They will often report control weaknesses to the board (usually via the Audit Committee) so that the board can improve these in the future.

Risk manager

The risk manager has specific responsibility for risk management in the organisation. Tasks and responsibilities include amongst others:

- Monitoring risk management activities based on the risk management model used on the organisation (e.g. COSO ERM model), and proposing improvements

- Prepare presentations for Board (including the risk and audit committees if present) updating them on risks in the business

- Improve and monitor risk reporting throughout the organisation

- Provide training throughout the business risk management

- Sharing of knowledge and best practices with the aim of embedding risk management within the culture of the organisation

- Develop cost effective and practical solutions in conjunction with management to improve the level of control and reduce risk exposure

Comparing the risk manager and the internal auditor: the risk manager is focused on identifying and managing the risks and risk management processes in the organisation including developing relevant controls, while the internal auditor's focus is on identifying controls the controls that already existing, assessing their effectiveness and suggesting improvements.

4. Control objectives

Internal control activities are designed to provide reasonable assurance that particular objectives are achieved, or related progress understood. The **specific target used to determine whether a control is operating effectively** is called the **control objective**.

For example, a **control objective** for the accounts payable function may be stated as: "Payments are made only for authorised products and services received." A typical **control procedure** designed to achieve this objective is: "The accounts payable system compares the purchase order, receiving record, and vendor invoice prior to authorising payment." For any particular control objective it is likely that many controls will be in place that in combination help to meet that objective. In the above case it may be that two staff members authorise payments so there is a double check on all payments made so no one person can commit a fraud.

5. Control activities or procedures

Control activities procedures are defined as **specific sets of policies, procedures, and activities designed to meet a control objective**.

Control activities may also be explained by the type or nature of activity. These include (but are not limited to) the SOAPSPIRT controls:

Segregation of duties - separating authorisation, custody, and record keeping roles of fraud or error by one person. This stops any one person having full control of an activity and stops them being able to commit a fraud without collaborating with others. It also means that any errors or problems may be spotted by others involved in the process.

Organisational – A clear organisational structure ensures that each key area of the business is managed effectively. Allocating responsibility for each area to key managers ensure someone is accountable for the performance of that area of the business.

Authorisation – review, check and authorisation by a more senior staff member helps find errors, ensure staff abide by policy and may identify and prevent frauds. e.g. authorisation of large purchases.

Processing or Accounting Controls – Includes specific controls over a process. Exactly what will depend on the process. For data entry for example it could be only allowing data meeting certain criteria to be allowed to be entered, such as all customer numbers being numbers only and 8 numbers in length. For accounting systems it would include controls such as bank reconciliations and ensuring the balance sheet balances.

Supervision or monitoring of operations - observation or review of ongoing operational activity ensures work is well planned and on track. Supervisors also control staff day to day to ensure they are doing what they are supposed to be doing as well as providing support, training and guidance.

Physical safeguards - usage of cameras, locks, physical barriers, etc. to protect property, such as merchandise inventory.

IT Controls – e.g. usage of passwords, access logs, virus checkers and so on to ensure IT security is well managed and IT systems effective.

Records retention - maintaining documentation and information to allow for audit and review

Top-level reviews - analysis of actual results versus organisational goals or plans, variance analysis, periodic and regular operational reviews, metrics, and other key performance indicators (KPIs).

6. Levels of control

There are 3 levels at which control can be applied:

Strategic level control

At the strategic level (the level of the organisation's directors), internal control objectives relate to the achievement of strategic goals and objectives. E.g. Strategic planning and review, organisational structures and procedures, governance arrangements, financial reporting, and overall compliance with laws and regulations.

Management level control

Managers run divisions and departments and need to control these. Typically the key focus at this level is providing key objectives and budgets to focus what the manager work towards, and reviewing performance against those objectives on a regular basis.

Operational control

At a lower, operational level, the level of the "workers" undertaking standard tasks, internal control refers to the actions taken to achieve a specific detailed task or objective e.g. standard manufacturing procedures, authorisation of transactions or security procedures.

7. Control precision and sufficiency

Control precision describes the alignment or correlation between a particular control procedure and a given control objective or risk. A control with direct impact on the achievement of an objective (or mitigation of a risk) is said to be more precise than one with indirect impact on the objective or risk.

Example: Locking a valuable diamond ring in a locked safe has high precision over the objective of keeping that asset safe. Keeping it in a shop window behind toughened glass, has medium precision. The ring is safe, but it's not completely so.

Precision is distinct from **sufficiency**; that is, multiple controls with varying degrees of precision may be involved in achieving a control objective or mitigating a risk.

Example: Locking the ring in the safe could also be deemed sufficient security if the risk of theft is fully mitigated. However, if we're going to keep that ring in the shop window being toughened glass we probably need a number of other controls in place before it's security is sufficient which might include; staff always present in the shop, locking the ring away overnight, CCTV cameras, locked window displays so there is no access from inside the shop.

Precision is an important factor in performing a risk assessment. After identifying specific risks management need to identify and test controls that mitigate the risks. This involves making judgements regarding both precision and sufficiency of controls required to mitigate the risks. Assurance mapping may be used as part of the process to map risks to controls.

8. Control weaknesses and compliance failures

Definition

It is vital that risks in the organisation are dealt with and the key method to deal with these is through controls. The key role of the internal audit department, where an organisation has one, is to review controls that are in place and identify **control weaknesses** and **compliance failures**, and to report back on these

A **control weakness** can include:

- risks have not been effectively controlled so the **net risk** remains high (remember net risk is risk after all controls and other mitigating factors have been applied). This is typically when there is:
    - a lack of **control precision** – individual controls have low do not fully deal with the risks they are trying to deal with.
    - a lack of **sufficiency** of controls – there are not enough controls to fully mitigate the risk
- **controls are in place**, but are not being applied correctly

A **compliance failure** is where the organisation has not abided by a regulation or law e.g. financial statements not produced according to accounting standards, health and safety laws are breached, or governance codes not abided by.

Method for evaluating controls

Following on directly from these definitions, in order to be able to evaluate controls and compliance failures we need to ask the following questions:

- What are the **key risks** in this organisation – considering risks strategically, operationally and as a breach of compliance?
- **What controls** are in place to mitigate the risks?
- What is the '**precision**' of those controls (i.e. how effective is each control?).
- Are there **sufficient controls** in place to fully mitigate the risk?
- Are the controls being **applied correctly**?

Finally, where there are weaknesses the organisation should ask: **What other controls** should be applied in this situation?

Example

Our jewellery shop owner employs 6 staff. Most members of staff were people he knows or in two cases just people who walked into the shop asking if any positions were available. Each employee has a clear employment contract with stated hours, policies and conditions. Training on internal procedures is given on the first day of them joining and after that they are allowed to man the shop and apply the security procedures, which are detailed and robust. Once in place the staff are allowed a lot of flexibility as the owner aims to ensure a relaxed friendly environment to work in and staff are happy. Staff have excellent attendance records and low sickness levels, although this relaxed approach and lack of supervision has, at times resulted in some of the security procedures not being followed. Sales levels from different staff vary greatly, the top sales people selling almost double those who do less well.

So let's evaluate some of the controls over staff.

Risk	Controls and their precision	Are they sufficient?	Are they being applied correctly?	What other controls would be useful?
Staff are not effective salespeople	Induction training (low precision as not enough about sales during induction)	No Very few controls in this area – significantly more needed	Yes Induction training does happen	Recruitment controls to recruit better sales people Sales training for each staff member Sales targets to focus staff work Regular staff appraisals for review and feedback
Security weaknesses	Security procedures in place (high)	Yes	No	Staff supervision Disciplinary action when not following rules
Risk that staff attendance is poor	Relaxed working environment (Medium) Clear contract (Medium)	Appears to be sufficient as attendance is good.	Yes	Disciplinary action for non-attendance

9. Internal control and Fraud

A **fraud** is an intentional deception made for personal gain or to damage another individual.

Internal control plays an important role in the prevention and detection of fraud. A **fraud risk assessment** helps to identify potential fraud risks and assess whether the related controls are sufficient to manage these risks.

This typically involves identifying scenarios in which theft or loss could occur and determining if existing control procedures effectively manage the risk to an acceptable level. The risk that senior management might override important financial controls to manipulate financial reporting is also a key area of focus in fraud risk assessment.

Ultimately it is **management's responsibility** to identify and manage fraud. External auditors are only responsible for finding significant frauds, that are material to the financial statements.

To help manage frauds many organisation have an **anti-fraud policy statement** which establishes ground rules which essentially clarify that fraud will not be tolerated and spells out the consequences. It can also include a **fraud response plan**, a framework for how the company will respond in the event of a fraud, and which will include items such as who and how it will be investigated, disciplinary procedures followed and a PR plan. The overall objective is to limit the organisation's exposure to fraud and to minimise financial loss and the potential adverse affects on its image and reputation in the event of its occurrence.

Controls are a key element in fraud prevention, in particular those over the money and finance, so that fraud is hard to commit or discovered quickly if it is. Typical controls include:

- Staff supervision

- Approval and authorisation (e.g. of payments made)

- Segregation of duties (so no one person has full control, so two people would have to collude to commit fraud)

- Accounting controls such as reconciliation (so that frauds are quickly identified)

- Strong recruitment procedures to ensure trustworthy and loyal staff with strong values of integrity and honesty are employed

- A culture (control environment) that stresses the importance of integrity and honesty

- Clear disciplinary procedures

10. Problems with internal control

Internal control problems

Assurance is not absolute

Internal control can provide reasonable, not absolute, assurance that the objectives of an organisation will be met. The concept of reasonable assurance implies a high degree of assurance. This must be weighed up against the additional costs or practicalities of increased assurance.

For example, security at a sporting event could be enhanced by not allowing spectators, but that would change the whole nature and purpose of the event. Security can never be 100% assured, but procedures can be put in place to ensure an acceptable level of security given the risks.

Some factors are out of the organisation's control

Effective internal control implies the organisation generates reliable financial reporting and substantially complies with the laws and regulations that apply to it. However, whether an organisation achieves operational and strategic objectives may depend on factors outside the enterprise, such as competition or technological innovation.

These factors are outside the scope of internal control; therefore, effective internal control provides only timely information or feedback on progress towards the achievement of operational and strategic objectives, but cannot guarantee their achievement.

Dependent on people

Controls are also highly dependent on people, and can often be overridden either on purpose (e.g. to commit a fraud) or by human error.

Bureaucracy and inflexibility

Controls can become a bureaucratic – a long series of reviews and checklists that take a lot of time to complete, and can serve to restrict innovation and flexibility.

The purchasing process for example could be long and cumbersome requiring tender documents, reviews, authorisation and supplier checks. This could delay the purchase and ultimately affect the end customer who may get the delivery of their product delayed.

Too many controls and too much bureaucracy in a hospital could delay a crucial operation or them receiving and important drug which could have severe consequences for the patient.

Costs

Implementing controls can be costly. The salaries of Non-executive directors are a classic example of a significant expense for staff that are present on the board mostly for control purposes. More simply the cost of quality control checks or spending more on safer equipment or training are all examples of the costs of controls.

Benefits vs costs

Ultimately the organisation needs to balance the benefits of increased risk management and control of the business with the practicalities of running the business efficiently and effectively. Control is good, but not when there is so much bureaucracy and too high a cost to the achievement of the organisation's ultimate goals.

CIMA P3 Course Notes

Chapter 5
Management Control Systems

1. Management control systems

Management control systems are tools to aid management for steering an organisation toward its strategic objectives and competitive advantage.

Robert N. Anthony (2007) defined Management Control is the process by which managers influence other members of the organisation to implement the organisation's strategies.

According to Maciariello et al. (1994), management control is concerned with coordination, resource allocation, motivation, and performance measurement.

2. Management control

Management control systems are implemented through the following management controls:

- organisational structure
- human resources management
- culture and ethics
- policies, procedures and processes.

Organisational structure

An organisational structure outlines the roles and responsibilities of individuals and groups within an organisation. An organisational structure consists of activities such as task allocation, coordination and supervision, which are directed towards the achievement of organisational aims.

Structure is used for management control as it provides:

- the foundation on which standard operating procedures and routines rest as these are often structured and controlled by a specific group.
- a focus for decision making – with clear decision making responsibilities allocated to department managers.
- functional or project responsibilities can be allocated to specific parts of the structure creating a **control centre** which is then responsible for control of a particular area of the business (e.g. financial control to the finance department).

Typical structures are how they relate to control:

Entrepreneurial

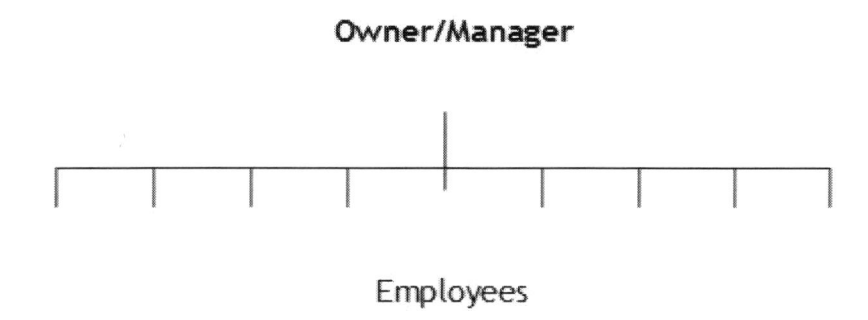

Owner/Manager

Employees

Control exercised by the leader, their expertise and the way they run and manage their staff directly.

Functional

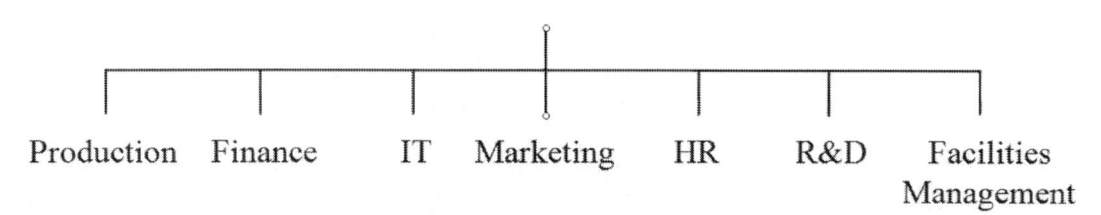

BOARD OF DIRECTORS

Production   Finance   IT   Marketing   HR   R&D   Facilities Management

In a functional structure, groups of experts work together to perform specified roles for the organisation. Control is exercised by functional responsibilities and functional experts.

From a management accounting perspective, each functional area is usually a **cost centre** to which individual budgets are allocated, and costs reviewed and controlled using variance analysis.

Divisional

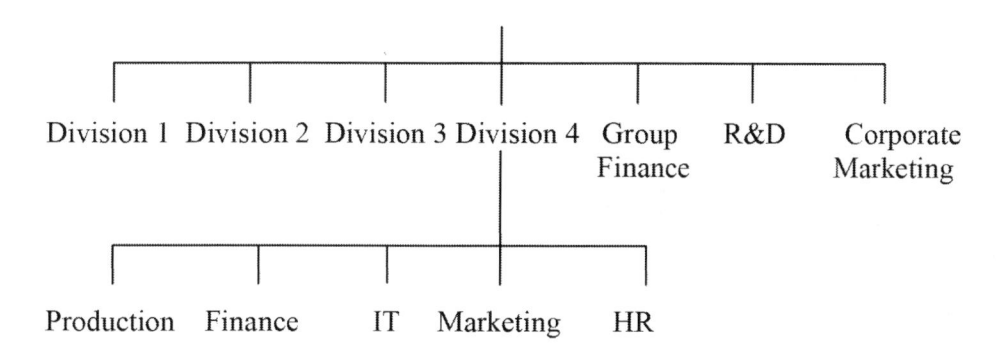

BOARD OF DIRECTORS

Division 1   Division 2   Division 3   Division 4   Group Finance   R&D   Corporate Marketing

Production   Finance   IT   Marketing   HR

Divisions can be based on product, customer or geographic groupings. Control is exercised by delegated managerial responsibility for each division.

Each division can controlled using profit based targets for division managers (**profit centre**). If the manager also controls investment divisions can be managed using Return on Investment (ROI) or Residual Income (RI measures as an **investment centre**.

Matrix

	Marketing	Finance	Production	Design
Customer A				
Customer B				
Customer C				
Customer D				

Often used in project environments to get more control over projects through better management and communication in project teams.

Network

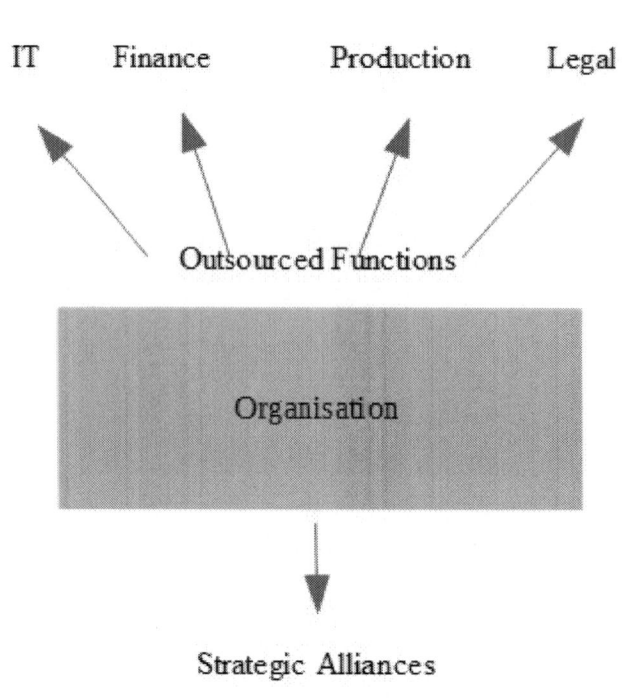

IT   Finance   Production   Legal

Outsourced Functions

Organisation

Strategic Alliances

Network organisations depend on the relationships with external organisations. Control is exercised mostly by well drafted and focused contracts (also called service level agreements or SLAs) including clear performance measurements and penalties for non-compliance. Relationships with partner companies are also key to control.

Human resources management

Human resource management (HRM, or simply HR) is the management of an organisation's workforce, or human resources. Organisational control is exercised by:

- Attracting and selecting suitably qualified staff
- Training to give people the right skills and attitudes to do the best work
- Rewarding of employees including incentive schemes
- Employment contracts, setting out clear expectations of role
- Setting and applying disciplinary procedures
- Ensuring staff satisfaction and motivation, leading to good productivity
- Performance appraisal to give feedback

Culture

Culture is defined by Charles Handy as "The way we do things around here".

Culture is a combination of the VANE factors:

- Values
- Attitudes
- Norms
- Expectations.

Individuals often act within the standard norms of group behaviour. If, for example, people generally work late it is likely that a new employee will see that this is the norm and do that too, even if this is not stated in the company's policies. Such cultural norms can have a dramatic effect on the organisation and success, and hence 'management control', particularly when such norms relate to attitudes to:

- working hard or long hours
- loyalty
- innovation

- quality
- customers
- meeting deadlines
- support for others.

Control over culture can be exercised through

- statement of values outlining what the organisation stands for
- training
- recruitment of staff with new beliefs, values or approaches
- senior management being seen to act in a new way
- new rules and procedures - clarifying expected behaviours
- new symbols (e.g. buildings, job titles, logos)
- changing groups and structures
- new reward systems encouraging new behaviour.

Policies, procedures and processes

Standard policies, procedures and processes ensure people know what is expected of them, and that they operate in a standard structured way. Their work is therefore 'controlled' within the bounds of the policy, procedure or process.

There are three types of business processes:

Management processes, the processes that govern the operation of a system. Typical management processes include "Corporate Governance" and "Strategic Management".

Operational processes, processes that constitute the core business and create the primary value stream. Typical operational processes are Purchasing, Manufacturing, Advertising and Marketing, and Sales.

Supporting processes, which support the core processes. Examples include Accounting, Recruitment, Call centre, Technical support.

Business Processes are designed to add value for the customer and should not include unnecessary activities. The outcome of a well designed business process is increased effectiveness (value for the customer) and increased efficiency (less costs for the company).

3. Management accounting control systems

One of the key methods of management control is the use of management accounting as a control tool.

What is management accounting?

Management Accounting is "the process of identification, measurement, accumulation, analysis, preparation, interpretation and communication of information used by management to plan, evaluate and **control** within an entity and to assure appropriate use of and accountability for its resources. Management accounting also comprises the preparation of financial reports for non-management groups such as shareholders, creditors, regulatory agencies and tax authorities" (CIMA Official Terminology).

Methods of accounting and their relationship to control

Management accounting method	What does it control?
Budgeting	- Spending - Business planning (assuming budgets link directly to overriding business plans and strategies)
Variance analysis	- Spending within budgeted limits - Efficiency (e.g. labour usage variance) - Wastage (e.g. Idle time variance)
Standard costing	- Spending within expected costs and efficiency levels
Investment analysis (NPV, IRR, Relevant costing)	- Investment decisions e.g. NPV ensures investments achieve the returns required to satisfy shareholders
Transfer pricing	- Market Control i.e. allows for managers to make their own decisions based on fair transfer prices - Ensures fairness within internally based pricing systems
Absorption, marginal and activity based costing	- Organisational or divisional profit - Sets a cost card that allows for control of pricing and costs

Responsibility accounting (Cost centres, Profit centres, Investment centres, ROCE)	• Controls functional and division managers by setting budgets and through performance measurement
Balanced scorecard	• Controls functional and divisional managers though non-financial as well as financial measures. The four areas are: Financial, Internal, Innovation and learning, Customer.
Breakeven analysis	• Investment decisions
Forecasting techniques, such as regression analysis and time series analysis	• Controls costs and business planning through more accurate budgeting and costing

Problems with use of management accounting techniques for control

Problems of management accounting include:

- The process is too long so investment decisions and business plans are delayed
- Cost of analysis
- There is a lot of game playing (e.g. over budgeting or investment decisions)
- Business decisions change but the budget does not
- People in charge of budget are held accountable in areas where they have no responsibility
- Inaccurate forecasting makes budgets inappropriate and investment analysis

4. Controlling Ethics

Ethics and social responsibility

Ethics are a code of moral principles that people follow with respect to what is right or wrong.

Examples might include

- treatment of workers
- avoiding bribery
- good professional conduct and honesty
- respecting people's personal data
- appropriate and fair advertising
- safety at work.

Social responsibility is the duty the organisation has towards the wider community or society. Examples might include

- supporting charity
- environmental issues
- public safety
- exploitation of third-world workers

Most modern organisations take the view that they, and their boards of directors, have a **duty of care to wider stakeholders to look after the interests of all stakeholders** from a moral perspective. That could mean spending more money (e.g. on safer equipment, or using more responsible suppliers) which may reduce profits in the short term. The board to therefore aim to balance ethical obligations with their fiduciary duty to provide shareholders with a good return on their investment. In the long term it can be argued that "good ethics is good business" as the reputational benefits can outweigh the short term costs.

Ethical Risks - Why are ethics important to the business?

The long and short of ethics is the idea of moral right and wrongs. An organisation should hold itself up to high moral standards for no other reason than they think it is the right thing to do.

However, as well as being morally right, being ethical also has business consequences, and those must be considered as key **ethical risks** from a business perspective. Ethical issues can have a number of advantages to the business:

- generate good feeling amongst staff
- avoid legal action
- avoid bad publicity and the potential damage to reputation which might result
- as a source of competitive advantage, as positive ethical behaviour can become a selling point and support the brand.

The public relations (PR) and other business consequences of any unethical behaviour must be considered alongside the moral rights and wrongs of that behaviour, although take care not to confuse the two. The point of ethical behaviour is to act in a way that is morally right, and that should be the driving force. PR consequences are an additional factor which must be considered on top of those moral rights and wrongs.

Ethics and risk management

Risk management ensures that the key risks involved in the business are well managed and controlled, and as such is a key element of corporate governance. As such risk management ensures that excessive risks are not taken and ensures shareholders returns are protected, employees jobs are safer, customers are more assured of continued supply of their product and creditors and suppliers more assured of a return of their money. A duty of care is owed to all these stakeholders and as such good risk management upholds the organisation's ethical duties.

Ethical control

There are three key ways to control ethics within an organisation:

1. **Personal ethics**

These are the moral principles held by individuals. The ethics of the organisation will closely reflect the ethics of its staff. This is particularly true of the senior management in an organisation since they make the significant decisions. They are also role models for other staff and so their behaviour may influence that of other staff.

Control over personal ethics can be exercised through employing people with suitable ethical principles. This might be through making it a part of the recruitment procedure through references being taken or checks on personal histories.

2. Organisational culture

The culture is the combination of the beliefs, values and standards of behaviour inherent in an organisation. Often behaviours are influenced by what is seen to be right or wrong within the group of employees. A group "ethical stance" may well develop which is adhered to by its members and perpetuated through others learning what is acceptable within the group.

Control can be exercised through:

- Statement of values outlining what the organisation stands for. Values such as integrity, fairness, truthfulness might encourage ethical approach to work.

- Communication of ethical expectations (e.g. on induction programmes).

- Senior management leading the way by behaving ethically themselves and supporting ethical behaviour in others.

3. Organisational systems

These are the sets of internal processes and activities which dictate the way the organisation operates. The development of organisational systems around ethical issues can facilitate ethical control. These could include

- reward systems - to reward good ethical behaviour

- recruitment systems - to recruit the right people

- ethical codes outlining strict behavioural rules to be followed

- ethical audits - a review of a department's ethical behaviour

- disciplinary procedures to be used when people break ethical rules.

5. CIMA Code of ethics

As we have seen earlier, one key method of ethical control is personal ethics. One driver of such personal ethical behaviour for professionals are ethical codes of conduct. The CIMA code is one good example of this and is applicable to CIMA members.

Fundamental Principles of CIMA code of Ethics

The CIMA code of ethics identifies **5 fundamental principles** to which a professional accountant should comply:

1. Integrity

This means being straightforward and honest in all professional and business relationships. The accountant should not be associated with information they believe contains a false or misleading statement, or which is misleading by omission. Integrity also means acting consistently.

For example, an accountant should not misstate information because they have been asked to do so by a superior is that information is not correct.

2. Objectivity

This means being unbiased and acting in an impartial manner. There should be no conflicts of interest or illicit relationships that might influence members in their professional or business judgements.

For example, an accountant should not accept (or offering) excessive hospitality from people with whom they might have to review their work as this could lead to bias creeping in or feelings of embarrassment, which might prejudice their independence.

3. Professional Competence and Due Care

This means ensuring that one's professional knowledge, skills and technical standards are maintained at the level required to practice with full competence. Keeping up to date with developments in practice, legislation and techniques. Any limitations in technical and professional standards should be disclosed and remedied. For example, attending professional courses to update knowledge of the latest accounting rules.

4. Professional Behaviour

This means avoiding actions that could discredit the profession, and complying with relevant laws and regulations. They should be honest and truthful.

For example, the accountant should not make exaggerated claims about their qualifications or the services they offer and should not make disparaging references to the work of others or say anything dishonest or untrue.

5. Confidentiality

This means respecting confidentiality and safeguarding information obtained through professional and business relationships. The accountant should not use information for their personal advantage. They should not disclose unauthorised information, acquired from professional relationships, to others outside the company or employing organisation. This includes breeching confidentiality in a social situation.

For example, you should not discuss a colleague's financial information with a family member.

The principle of confidentiality continues even after a business relationship has been terminated.

Disclosure

The exception to maintaining confidentiality is when there is **a legal or professional right or duty to disclose.** CIMA's code of conduct lists the particular circumstances in which confidential information could be disclosed. They are:

- Where disclosure is **required by law**, such as in a case of legal infringement

- Where disclosure is **permitted by law,** such as during a legal investigation where one is protecting one's professional interests

- Where disclosure is authorised by a client or employer

- Where disclosure is professionally permissible

6. Controlling Quality

There are 3 key methods of managing quality in an organisation, quality control, quality assurance and Total Quality Management (TQM).

Quality Control

Quality control is the process of ensuring that the quality of goods meets set standards. The following process is usually used:

- Set quality standards
- Set procedures and production processes to deliver these standards
- Measure actual quality produced
- Discard rejects or rectify problems identified
- Change the process if products are consistently below quality standards.

Quality Assurance

Quality assurance aims to reduce the amount of quality checking that occurs by have good internal processes and procedures which guarantee the quality of the final products. This might for instance include:

- Using machinery that is a high quality
- Training staff to a high level
- Getting suppliers to guarantee the quality of goods supplied (this avoids the costs of quality checks on receiving goods)

Total Quality Management (TQM)

TQM is the principle of a culture of quality throughout the whole organisation. Quality is a key strategic focus. TQM has a number of key principles:

- Errors and defects should be prevented, the costs of prevention being less than the costs of correction – part of **'Getting things right first time'**
- The aim is to achieve **no defects**
- Continuous improvement
- Quality should be a concern of the whole organisation not just production.

Quality management like this can be applied to a management accounting function, with the aim that management accounting information should be 'right first time' and 'continuously improved' with the focus on the organisation's needs for better quality information.

To achieve these goals in a management accounting function the department might include:

- Training staff (e.g. CIMA qualification, excel training)
- Communication mechanisms being put in place to encourage the sharing of ideas – both with the users of the information and the finance staff themselves
- Processes are redesigned for quality (e.g. excellent finance systems which are tested and checks and have internal controls built in them)
- Use of reconciliations and checks
- Supervision and review of all information produced

Cost of quality

There are four key costs associated with quality. We will link each of these to what these would be for a management accounting department aiming for high quality levels:

Prevention costs – costs associated with preventing errors (e.g. training costs, using qualified staff, excellent IT systems)

Appraisal costs – costs associated with the review of information to check for errors and problems (e.g. management accounting manager salary).

Internal failure costs – costs when an error is made within the department (e.g. costs of staff recalculating numbers after an error is made).

External failure costs – costs associated with errors after information has left the department. These could include the costs of poor decisions made by managers using information that is not correct.

7. Lean Production and Management

Born out of competition between Japanese and Western countries; lean production is essentially the act of **cutting all non-value adding** parts of the business from the value chain; or in layman's terms achieving the same outcome from less work and cost. A lean production system will integrate all employees, managers and suppliers together working together towards the same goal and remove any people, processes and parts that do not support that goal.

One element of lead production is the removal of waste. According to the Toyota Production System there are details seven key areas of waste:

Transport - When an item or machine is unnecessarily moved when this movement plays no part in production. For example, you build your car bodies in one room but attach the wheels next door. The time to transport between buildings adds no value to the product and so should be removed from the process.

Inventory - When raw materials, finished products or works in progress are unnecessarily in stock; this should not happen under lean production as excess or stationary inventory adds no value to the product. Lean production systems use a Just-In-Time inventory system.

Motion - People or machines being moving more than is/should be required; for example, you are a mechanic working on a car production line and your job is to check and correct any default in the engine. However, every default requires different tools and the tools must be kept in another room, as a result at lease once an hour you have to make a 2 minute round trip to the next room. This is an example of motion that is not beneficially to the product and so is a waste. If this happened just once an hour you would waste an hour and twenty minutes a week!

Waiting - Any time a product, person or machine is left waiting to complete their task is not adding value to the product. To return to our car example, any time a worker completes their task on a car, a new car should be rolling into their station. If they have to wait for whatever reason that is wasted time, that employees time adds no value to the end product during that time and so steps will need to be taken to ensure waiting time is reduced.

Overproduction - When more stock is produced than needed, the excess stock will need space to occupy, tie up unnecessary capital and risk stock obsolescence. Our cars, unlike a fine wine, will not appreciate in value by being stuck in a warehouse and as a result this storage is not adding anything to the cars production and value, therefore any overproduction needs to stop.

Over processing - Another perhaps slightly confusing waste, essentially it means that more quality or extras added to a product do not necessarily mean consumers will value it more. For example, if our cars target market only want a cheap little run around yet we have spent time and money installing the most expensive branded tyres, in the eyes of our consumers we have not added any value to the car; they will NOT be willing to pay more for these tyres. Therefore the time and money these tyres cost over standard non branded ones is a waste as they did not contribute value to the customer.

Defects - Defects often cost far more than people think; in addition to the added costs/time needed to repair the product (or scrap if necessary) we must also include the materials that went into the product, the cost of the machines/personnel who made it and the cost of the products that would have been made in its place. Often the true cost of a defect can be up to 10 times what it appears to initially have cost, particularly if it happens after the customer has received the product where not only are their cost implications but reputation implications also.

Criticisms and limitations of Lean Production

As with most forms of production, there are several pitfalls to the seeming ideal notion of lean production.

Many critics of lean production site management's focus solely on the tools and methodologies of lean, rather than the philosophy and culture. For example, if you work on a production line where you are constantly being hounded for wastes that fall into the seven areas, but you have no idea why you too would react negatively, and that is why managers need to install a culture of 'lean' within an organisation so that workers are aware of it and could in fact attempt to contribute to it.

Capacity can often be an issue for companies using 'lean production' as they are often working at close to full capacity (every input utilised - anything less would be a waste), however, by not having a surplus of materials, stock and personnel the company can be left high and dry if a massive order comes in out of the blue or there is suddenly a shortage of raw materials.

In other words, for lean production to work effectively, everything needs to keep running smoothly, as there is little to no room for any contingencies.

8. Controls by department

Each department needs to have controls to manage their area of operation. There can be many many controls for any department, and the key in exam questions is to ensure that any control that is suggested specifically deals with the risks in that case. However, let's look at a few of the most common controls for each department:

Sales department

Controls include:

- Sales targets for the department
- Sales targets for individual staff
- Staff recruitment controls to attract good candidates
- Staff appraisals
- Staff training programmes
- Controls over expenses
    - Supported by receipts
    - Set limits on expenditure for specific items
    - Manager review of claims

Purchasing department

Controls include:

- All purchases supported by an authorised purchase order
- Set limits for authorisation of certain amounts by agreed staff (e.g. amounts over £1,000 to be signed off by a director)
- Set processes for tendering
- Authorised suppliers only to be used
- Authorised catalogues of items only allowed
- Budgets for each department and item category, reviewed regularly against actual amounts spent (e.g. variance analysis)
- Robust IT systems which have been tested and include built in controls

Treasury function

The treasury function is responsible for working capital management and financing in an organisation.

Controls include:

- Regular cashflow forecasts
- Supervisor authorisation of key transactions e.g. foreign exchange contracts
- Overdrafts and flexible financing to allow for unexpected cash needs
- Staff recruitment processes – knowledgeable qualified staff
- Staff training
- Robust IT systems which have been tested and include built in controls
- Non-recourse factoring – where the factoring company takes the risk of the bad debt
- Credit insurance against bad debts

Distribution/Stores

Controls include:

- Regular stock-takes to review actual quantities against those reported on the system – differences should be investigated and causes found and rectified.
- All purchases linked to purchase orders and goods received notes
- All receipts and deliveries reviewed and checked
    - quantities
    - quality
- All deliveries signed for by customer
- Robust IT systems which record all stock in and stock out, and which have been tested and include built in controls
- Staff recruitment processes – trustworthy staff
- Staff training
- Delivery vehicles monitored (E.g. using telematics and GPS tracking).

HR department

Human resource management (HRM, or simply HR) is the management of an organisation's workforce, or human resources. Organisational control is exercised by:

- Attracting and selecting suitably qualified staff
- Training to give people the right skills and attitudes to do the best work
- Rewarding of employees including incentive schemes
- Employment contracts, setting out clear expectations of role
- Setting and applying disciplinary procedures
- Ensuring staff satisfaction and motivation, leading to good productivity
- Performance appraisal to give feedback

IT department

You must also be aware of IT controls, but these are dealt with in their own chapter.....

9. Risks in control systems

As you can see there are a wide range of different control systems which can be applied to the business. In this chapter we have reviewed:

- Structural control
- HR control
- Cultural control
- Processes and policies
- Quality control
- Management accounting control systems
- Controls by department
    - Purchasing
    - Sales
    - HR
    - Treasury

- Distribution/stores

There are **two key risks in control systems**:

- The control system does not **adequately manage the risks** of the process, department or organisation as a whole (they are not 'precise' (i.e. not focused on meeting the control objectives) or 'sufficient' (when combined they do not fully manage the risk)

- The controls in place are **not properly applied**

As such controls and controls systems need to be regularly reviewed and updated to ensure they remain relevant and tested to ensure those in place actually are being applied and work.

The **internal audit department** are specifically tasked with documenting and testing controls throughout the organisation. **Managers of departments** must also take responsibilities for control of their area of work too though and should regularly review the efficacy of the controls and make appropriate changes to keep them up to date.

Whether the combination of all controls in the organisation adequately control the risks in the business is the responsibility of the **board of directors** as a whole, although often that responsibility is delegated to the **audit committee** or **risk committee**.

CIMA P3 Course Notes

Chapter 6
Performance measurement

1. Control theory, performance targets and feedback

Control theory

Control theory is the basic underlying theory of controlling systems. The process of controlling according to control theory is as follows:

1. Setting performance standards.
2. Measurement of actual performance.
3. Comparing actual performance with standards.
4. Analysing deviations.
5. Correcting deviations.

Let's look at an example of an organisation aiming to 'control' profits....

1. Setting performance standards = annual profit target
2. Measurement of actual performance = accounting system used to measure actual results
3. Comparing actual performance with standards = probably summarised by the accounting department and reported to the board of directors for review
4. Analysing deviations – probably reviewed by the board of directors
5. Correcting deviations – decisions made on response to take (e.g. how to turn around a lower than expected profit) and action taken.

By repeating the process year in, year out, the organisations profits are controlled, and hopefully increased by setting continually improving profit targets and and learning from actual performance each year.

Control theory and performance target setting

One key element of control theory that can be directly applied to organisations is setting of appropriate **performance targets**, both for the whole division or department, or for individuals.

For departments targets could include:

- Financial – e.g. profits, cashflows, return on capital employed
- Customer focused e.g. customer satisfaction, number of complaints

- Internal focused e.g. efficiency levels and productivity
- Learning and innovation e.g. revenue from new products

Measures should also be chosen that are appropriate to that division or department e.g sales targets for the sales team, and staff skill level targets for HR.

An inappropriate target will drive performance towards inappropriate behaviour, so for example there have been examples of police forces who were measured on number of crimes solved who then diverted resources to simple buy easy to solve crimes in order to achieve targets at the expense of focusing on more important crimes for society.

Critically targets must be SMART:

- Specific so they are clear and understandable
- Measurable – so they can be objectively reviewed
- Achievable and realistic – or they will not be motivating
- Controllable by the manager with responsibility for achieving them
- Relevant to the organisation (e.g. linked to the organisation's objectives) and the individual responsible for achieving them so they can control whether the achieve the target or not.
- Timebound, so we know when to review them.

Management accounting and control theory

Management accounting techniques often apply control theory. Techniques such as budgeting, responsibility accounting, standard costing and the balanced scorecard focus on target setting. Variance analysis is a classic approach to analysing differences and identifying reasons for those differences, although it often comes to management to action the change

Feedback and performance appraisal

Feedback is a critical component of a control system. It is the comparison between actual results and objectives that provides feedback that in turn that determines the actions to be taken.

In business and accounting feedback is a very common element of control, for example:

- Staff performance appraisals and review
- Review of strategic plans
- Variance analysis and review of budgets against actual costs

- Performance measurement techniques such as the balanced scorecard

Positive feedback is where the feedback is good (i.e. profits are higher than budget) and our aim to learn why and retain these improvements. **Negative feedback** is where feedback is bad (e.g. profits are lower than budget) where the aim to learn why and correct this.

Incentive systems

To ensure target setting and appraisal works effectively managers should be rewarded for good performance, for instance through a bonus scheme based on achieving their targets, or though future promotion. Without this incentive the targets set may simply be ignored and become meaningless.

2. Types of responsibility centres

Performance targets are typically allocated to specific managers in control of specific departments in the organisation. These 'departments' in accounting terms are called 'responsibility centres', which means the areas of the business where one manager is responsible for a particular budget

There are four main types of responsibility centres, cost centres, revenue centres, profit centres and investment centres. Let's look at each.

Cost centres

A cost centre is a responsibility centre to which only costs are attributed (and not earnings or capital). For example, an organisation may consider its customer service division to be a cost centre. The organisation will use this centre to 'collect' customer service costs, making it easy to determine the cost per cost unit. For example, if the overhead to run the customer service centre is £10,000 for the period, and the centre deals with 1,000 customer queries, then the organisation can conclude the cost per query is £10.

Revenue centres

A revenue centre is a responsibility centre that is focused solely on generating revenue. A good example of this may be a fund-raising department of a not-for-profit, or a sales department of a commercial organisation. These centres will allocate all their resources to achieving the highest revenue possible, without any link to the associated costs.

Profit centres

A profit centre is a responsibility centre where the manager has autonomy over both costs and revenue. An example might be a particular store or region, operated by a single manager as a standalone unit. Obviously these centres are more involved than simple cost and revenue centres, as the manager must control both facets in order to achieve a good result.

Investment centres

An investment centre is a responsibility centre that is responsible for both costs and revenues, as well as the investment in assets used to support the division. The manager will therefore be responsible for supporting itself through sound asset disposals and acquisitions, as well as running a profitable operation. Dividing an organisation into investment centres is a heavy form of decentralisation – in effect, each unit of the business operates with its own management as an independent business unit. For this reason, investment centres are also commonly known as Strategic Business Units (SBUs).

3. Performance measurement of responsibility centres

Using appropriate performance measures

Due to the difference in the departments and what their managers are responsible for, each type of responsibility centre should be appraised on a different basis, so for example cost centre managers on spending against budget, while profit centre managers can also be appraised on profit.

It is important to appraise managers on the right managers in the right way to ensure they are motivated and achieving the goals of the company as a whole. Performance measurement is most effective when:

- There is goal congruence, i.e. the goals of the company and the goals of the centre's manager are aligned.

- Only aspects which can be controlled by the manager are evaluated. Items that are uncontrollable should be disregarded or clearly segregated in reports. This falls in line with the concept of responsibility accounting.

- Both long term and short term objectives are considered. This generally requires both financial and non-financial performance measures.

- Managers and divisions are evaluated separately. High performing managers may be in control of particularly weak divisions and vice versa. The performance of the division is not always a direct reflection of the manager in charge.

Performance measures for cost centres

The simplest form of measuring performance of a responsibility centre is a comparison between budget and actual results. This will measure the manager's ability to control costs and generate revenue. This is the typical measure used in cost centres.

In addition they may also use non-financial measures such as:

- Efficiency and productivity measures (e.g. transactions processed per hour)
- Learning and innovation e.g. amount spent on training, or number of new ideas implemented

Performance measures for revenue centres

In revenue centres the key measure is revenue. A sales department, for instance has, as their key focus achieving sales so that should be their main goal.

Revenue centres also incur some costs, staff salaries for instance, and as such can also be measured against costs incurred versus budget.

They may also have non-financial measures too. For a sales department that might be:

- Brand awareness
- Percentage of sales calls resulting in a sale
- Average sales per sales call

Performance measures for profit centres

Profit centres have the advantage of being both revenue generating and incurring costs and the main measure is then profit. Profit targets will encourage managers to balance incurring more costs with generating more revenues.

The can also have pure revenue and cost targets and budgets if appropriate, but if the ultimate goal of the organisation is profit then this is the better overall measure.

Profit centres can have non-financial measures too such as:

- Customer focused e.g. customer satisfaction, number of complaints
- Internal focused e.g. efficiency levels and productivity
- Learning and innovation e.g. revenue from new products

Performance measures for investment centres

Investment centres require a slightly more thorough approach. This is because managers of these centres are given the responsibility to oversee both profit and level of capital investment. While the profit, revenue, cost and non-financial measures discussed for early sections are still relevant there are even better measures that will assess profits in relation to the required investment. Detailed below are some common methods:

Return on Investment (ROI)

Undoubtedly you have heard of this measure in your studies before, as it is widely used and accepted around the world. The formula is as follows:

$$ROI = \frac{\text{Operating profit before tax}}{\text{Net Operating assets}}$$

A basic example may be as follows:

	Centre A	Centre B
Sales	£20,000	£100,000
Profit before tax	£5,000	£50,000
Assets	£25,000	£400,000
ROI	20%	12.5%

Advantages of ROI

- **Easy to understand** – useful for performance measures for non-financial managers and reporting to directors without a financial background.

- It is a percentage based measure which **allows comparability between different centres.** Notice in the example above that although centre B has a higher profit, it's ROI is much lower as they are not making as good use of their assets.

- Relates profit to the level of investment in the centre and so is better than profit alone.

Disadvantages of ROI

- It is based on net assets, which can fluctuate depending on which point the centre is in their asset life cycle (older assets will have depreciated and so have lower asset values). It can also deter management to invest for the long term, as large investments will reduce their ROI in the short term.

- Managers may be reluctant to take on any projects which return lower than the current ROI. In trying to keep the ROI as high as possible, they forgo projects that would increase the centre's overall profit, albeit at a lower rate of return.

- Can **be short-termist in** nature as it is often measured on a monthly, quarterly or annual basis which causes managers to focus on **short term profits to the detriment of the long term** (e.g. not spending money on training to increase annual profits but potentially leaving the department with a skills shortage)

Let's look at an example of that second point:

Let's say a new project costs £20,000 in investment and returns £3,000 profits a year. Let's look at how each cost centre would end up if they did this project:

	Centre A	Centre B
Profit before tax	£8,000	£53,000
Assets	£45,000	£420,000
ROI	17.8%	12.6%
Change	↓	↑

Note here then how centre B's ROI has gone up, they would do the project, while Centre A's has gone down so that manager would not.

This is what is known as **'dysfunctional behaviour'**, which is where the managers act in a way that is right for them given their 'measure' but not right for the organisation as a whole. In this case if the company might want project to go ahead but the managers are taking different views, not because of what is right for the company but because of they way their division is measured.

Residual Income (RI)

Residual income is different from ROI in that it produces an absolute figure rather than a percentage. When using this metric, managers are usually encouraged to achieve the highest residual income figure possible, and this **helps avoid dysfunctional behaviour**. It is calculated as follows:

RI = Profit – Capital charge (where capital charge = Assets x Cost of Capital)

Let's go ahead and calculate the RI of Centre's A and B to see how they compare. We'll assume a cost of capital of 10%.

	Centre A	Centre B
Profit before tax	£5,000	£50,000
Capital charge (Assets x 10%)	£2,500	£40,000
Residual income	£2,500	£10,000

As can be seen here, the ROI of Centre A is significantly higher than that of Centre B. However, Centre B has a higher RI, meaning it contributes more to the organisation's overall profit.

Let's return to our earlier example to show how RI helps prevent dysfunctional behaviour.

Remember that the new project costs £20,000 in investment and returns £3,000 profits a year. Let's look at how each cost centre would end up if they did this project:

	Centre A	Centre B
Profit before tax	£8,000	£53,000
Assets	£45,000	£420,000
Capital charge (Assets x 10%)	£4,500	£42,000
RI	3,500	11,000
Change	⬆	⬆

RI will encourage both managers to take on the project as it returns more than the 10% costs of capital. This is **'goal congruent' behaviour** where divisional managers make decisions that are right for the organisation as a whole.

The central management must also be careful with that approach though, as Centre A simply may not have the same opportunities for expansion as Centre B or be much newer so has not had the time to grow, yet Centre B's RI is much higher than Centre As. In that case, RI based performance measurement would simply be unfair on the manager of A not because of his poor performance but simply because she's managing a smaller division, and would likely alienate the manager of Centre A.

This demonstrates the issue of goal congruence and aligning the interest of managers and shareholders as a central issue in good performance measurement.

Advantages of RI

- Focused on maximising shareholder wealth by maximising profit while taking into account investment, so is better than profit alone.

- Cost of capital can be altered to reflect risk (higher risk divisions can have a higher cost of capital used).

Disadvantages of RI

- Produces an absolute figure which reduces comparability between units. A large centre like Centre B will tend to have a higher RI than one like Centre A, despite not using their assets as well. ROI gives a much better comparison.

- Like ROI, it is based on net assets, which can fluctuate depending on which point the centre is in their asset life cycle (older assets will have depreciated and so have lower asset values). It can also deter management to invest for the long term, as large investments will reduce their RI in the short term.

- Can be short-termist in nature as it is often measured on a monthly, quarterly or annual basis which causes managers to focus on short term profits to the detriment of the long term (e.g. not spending money on training to increase annual profits but potentially leaving the department with a skills shortage)

4. Balanced Scorecard

One of the problems of 'dysfunctional behaviour' is caused by too much focus on narrow financial measures (ROI for instance) which are the measured in the short term, causing managers to be too focused on short term profits at the expense of the long term.

Kaplan and Norton developed the balance scorecard which outlined four key areas in which company and divisional performance should be measured. The key idea is that managers to be appraised on a variety of measures which include non-financial measures so that their focus is both long and short term.

For example should a manager decide to delay training spend to increase annual profits, the result may be a lower 'spend on annual training' target and so the benefits of higher profits are countered by the poor performance on that measure. Similarly spending less on R&D could result in worse performance on a measure focused on development spend or number of new products released.

The 4 perspectives and suitable performance measures in each are:

Customer perspective

Focusing on the customer and meeting their needs.

Possible measures:

- Customer satisfaction - per a customer satisfaction survey
- Number of returns
- Number of customers moving to the competition.
- Call waiting time / service time
- Delivery time
- % of deliveries on time.

Internal business perspective

Focusing on the way the business works and operates with a particular focus on productivity and efficiency.

Measures include:

- Time per unit

- Number of defective products
- Cost per unit
- Material wastage rates

Innovation and learning perspective

Focusing on innovating in product and processes, and developing and learning for the future. Learning is more than just training, but includes any kind of organisational improvements made.

Measures include:

- No of new products developed
- Sales from new products
- Development time of new products
- R & D spending
- Amount spent per employee on training
- Number of qualified staff
- Number of training programmes available

Financial

Financial performance remains vital to the organisation's success, as it gives an indicator of shareholder wealth and ability to survive long term, and so must also be balanced against the other factors.

Measures include:

- Profits
- Return on investment
- Residual income
- Costs (variance analysis)
- Sales

Linked to strategy

In each category the organisation must follow through from the business' strategy, to ensure they are focused on the long term direction of the business.

Clear objectives should be set under each category according the SMART criteria (Specific, Measurable, Achievable, Relevant and Timebound), measured at the end of the period, and lessons learnt from actual results to help to improve performance in future periods and keep the organisation on track to achieve its strategic goals.

5. Transfer pricing

What is transfer pricing?

Imagine that you are the manager of an investment centre for a toy car company. The centre you manufactures engines.

A colleague of yours, let's call him Jim, also manages an investment centre for the same company. Jim manages the body centre, which takes all the different parts of the car and puts them together.

As both your centres are part of the same company, Jim is instructed to purchase his engines from you. Similarly, you are encouraged to supply him with the engines he needs.

However, with regards to performance measurement, you need to ensure that your centre is returning a profit. Therefore you are reluctant to 'sell' your engines to Jim at cost price, as this will only leave you at breakeven or maybe even a loss.

Conversely, Jim does not wish to purchase engines from you at market price, as he believes it is nonsensical to pay so much for goods being transferred to him from within the same company.

This scenario is what raises the issue of **transfer pricing**. Whenever divisions within the same organisation transfer goods to one another, they must determine a value for the goods for reporting purposes. This value is known as the **transfer price**, which, as you can see above is not always an easy value to agree upon. Every manager wishes to send or receive transfers at the best price possible to enhance his/her division's performance. The method to be used will often depend on the organisation's transfer pricing policy and the goals of the organisation.

6. Calculating a transfer price

A good transfer pricing system should aim to achieve the following:

- Optimal allocation of resources.
- Goal congruence.
- Motivate managers.
- Provide fair outcomes with regards to performance measurement.
- Retain the autonomy and independence of each division.
- Be simple to understand and not require frequent revisions.

As a general rule, transfer prices will fall within two limits:

Minimum transfer price – The minimum that a division will sell a unit for should amount to cost price plus any opportunity cost for selling the unit internally. In our above example, if an engine cost £50 to manufacture, and transferring it internally will result in profits foregone of a further £20, the minimum transfer price would amount to £70.

Maximum transfer price – The maximum price a division will pay for an internal transfer will amount to the lowest price that the unit could be acquired for from other suppliers. In our above example, if an engine was available to be bought on the open market for £80, then the maximum Jim would pay for engines internally would also be £80.

In the above scenario, the transfer price would then need to fall between £70 and £80. This is because you would not sell an engine for less than £70, as you could receive a higher price selling elsewhere, and similarly, Jim would not purchase an engine for over £80, as he could purchase cheaper engines in the marketplace.

Cost-based transfer pricing

To illustrate the different cost calculations, we'll refer to the following example:

Variable cost per engine	£40
Fixed overhead cost per engine	£10
Total cost per engine	£50
Normal mark-up	£20
Market price	£70
Production Capacity	100,000 units

Marginal cost

We can assume that marginal cost amounts to the variable cost of a unit. In this case, the transfer price would be £40.

Divisions will supply goods at marginal cost if there is no opportunity cost in doing so. Usually this will only occur when a division has excess capacity. Using our above example, you have the capacity to produce 100,000 units. If your demand only amounted to 60,000, there would be no opportunity cost to you if you were to supply Jim the remaining 40,000 engines at marginal cost. No sales would be lost, the cost of the extra units would be covered and Jim would get his supply at an attractive rate. If, however, your demand was at or over your 100,000 unit capacity, you would have a strong disincentive to supply Jim at anything less than the market price.

Absorption cost

In this case the transfer price would be £50 per engine (variable cost plus fixed overhead per unit). You would be happy to sell units at this price, but only if there was excess capacity to spare. However your incentive to sell in this situation is a little higher than before, as you will receive at least some contribution towards fixed costs.

Regardless, the market will still give you a higher selling price.

If absorption cost is used as a transfer price, there is also the possibility that the buying division can find a cheaper price from an outside supplier. For example, if Jim could purchase an engine elsewhere for £45 he would do it, as it's cheaper than the transfer price of £50.

From a big picture perspective this is a poor use of company resources - a division is paying an external party £45 for a product which can be produced internally for £40.

You may recall one of the conditions of a good transfer pricing system was optimal resource allocation, and in this scenario that is not being achieved. While Jim's division is saving money, the organisation is losing money as a whole.

One must also remember that this is only true in the event of spare capacity. If the selling division is selling its full capacity at market price (£70), the £20 profit it would earn per unit would outweigh the £5 loss described above, which leads to an overall positive outcome for the group as a whole.

Standard cost

One problem with using marginal cost or absorption cost as a transfer price is that the transferor is able to pass on cost overruns to the transferee. There is little incentive to keep costs down, as the marginal cost, however high it turns out to be, is paid for in full anyway by the buying party.

Using standard cost as a transfer price is therefore considered one of the more equitable options.

Standard cost does not take into account what actual costs are. Any adverse variance rests on the shoulders of the transferor, meaning that the transfer price is fixed at a fair level for both parties.

Two part tariff

This is the same as the marginal costing method, except the buying division is also required to pay a fixed annual fee. This fee represents a contribution towards the selling divisions fixed costs, as well as a payment for the privilege of receiving transfers at the lowest possible price.

This approach works well because both divisions are able to receive some benefit from the intra-company transfer.

Market-based transfer pricing

When an organisation is decentralised it is encouraged that they operate as standalone business units, with managers in charge of all aspects of the operation. Under this reasoning, market-based transfer prices would be the most suitable. After all, if the division really was an autonomous business unit, the open market is where they would need to go to for supply.

The key issue with this approach is determining a true 'market cost'. This can prove difficult for the following reasons:

- Different suppliers quote different prices
- Different buyers command different prices (including discounts, credit terms etc.)
- Current market prices may fluctuate or be seasonal
- Internal transfers reduce the need for advertising, sales staff and delivery costs, therefore the market price may benefit the transferor more than expected
- The product may not be available on the open market

Dual pricing

In most cases, using marginal cost as a transfer price will maximise the profit of the group as a whole. This is because units are transferred at the lowest price possible, allowing the buying divisions to maximise their output and keep costs as low as possible.

The problem with this approach is that the selling divisions do not recognise any profit on internal transfers, which provides little motivation for the division to supply the product a. It also undercuts their ability to operate as a standalone business unit, which is the reason organisations tend to decentralise in the first place.

To address these issues, an organisation may resort to a dual pricing method of transfer pricing. As the name suggests, this system uses two prices:

- The transferor is credited at a price that is equal to total cost, plus a mark-up.

- The transferee is debited at marginal cost.

Using two prices has two key advantages. First, the transferor is able to record a profit on each transfer. This provides an incentive for the manager in charge to supply.

Secondly, the transferee is able to obtain goods at marginal cost. This means they receive the lowest possible price, which maximises output and sales, which in turn maximises the group's overall profit.

You may have already noticed that this approach doesn't quite add up from an accounting standpoint; the debits and credits on each transfer do not match. To remedy this, the difference is debited to a group account known as a transfer pricing adjustment account. This amount is subtracted from the group's overall profit at the end of the period to ensure the accounts remain in balance.

Despite these advantages, dual pricing is rarely used. It is a complicated and time consuming method, especially when a high volume of goods are being transferred between multiple divisions.

Negotiated transfer prices

It is sometimes accepted that in a truly autonomous system where business units operate independently, transfer prices should be simply agreed on by the managers themselves. The assumption here is if the business units are truly operating autonomously, the managers should be competent to negotiate suitable prices for themselves.

While this approach might sound simple there are various weaknesses that need to be considered:

- Negotiations can be time consuming and drawn out.

- The managers may not be able to reach an agreement, in which case central management will need to intervene, undermining the managers' ability to operate autonomously.

- One manager may be more experienced or more dependent on the other, leading to a negotiation that is unfair.

Profit maximising transfer prices

Ideally, an organisation would want managers to use transfer prices that maximise the profit of the group as a whole. However, as we've already discussed, transfer prices that are best for the group and transfer prices that are best for each division are rarely the same. The challenge therefore is encouraging managers to use transfer prices that maximise both the profit of the group and their individual divisions. As we'll see in the example below, this is not always straightforward.

Example:

Toy Cars Ltd has two divisions.

The Engine Division produces engines. The Body Division manufactures toy cars, each of which include one engine.

The Engine Division

At a price of £60 there is no demand, but demand increases by 6 units for every £3 decrease in price. The variable cost of producing an engine is £12. There are no capacity constraints.

The Body Division

At a price of £80 there is no demand, but demand increases by 50 cars for every £10 decrease in price. The marginal cost of a car is £18 (not including the cost of the engine).

We are given the following equations to calculate price and marginal revenue:

$P = a - bx$

$MR = a - 2bx$

You should also remember that profit is maximised at the point where **marginal revenue is equal to marginal cost**.

We can look at this from two perspectives. First, we'll see what the results would be if the transferor acted in their own best interest and aimed to maximise their own profit, regardless of the effect on the group as a whole.

Profit maximisation for the transferor

Remember the equation for price is as follows:

$P = a - bx$

We can see that the price starts at £60 per unit, and every time it falls by £3 demand increases by 6 units. We can simplify this to say that demand increases by 1 unit for every £0.5 decrease in price.

Mathematically, the equation can then be defined as follows:

P = 60 - 0.5x

As was provided, the equation for marginal revenue is as follows:

MR = a – 2bx

Therefore,

MR = 60 – 1x

We also know that profit is maximised when marginal revenue is equal to marginal cost (MC = MR), which as we know from the information provided, is £12. Therefore;

12 = 60 – x

x = 48

Now that we've discovered our quantity, let's plug it into our price equation to find our point of profit maximisation:

P = 60 – 0.5x

P = 60 -24

P = 36

Therefore our **profit maximising price in the Engine Division** will be £36 per engine.

Now that we know the price of engines, we can see how this would affect the Body Division and the organisation as a whole.

We know that the demand for cars increases by 50 for every £10 decrease in price. We can simplify this to say that demand increases by 1 unit for every £0.2 decrease in price. Using the same price equation (P = a – bx), we can express this as follows:

P = 80 - 0.2x

Therefore, because MR = a – 2bx,

MR = 80 – 0.4x

We also know that the marginal cost of producing a car is as follows:

MC = £18 (given) plus £36 (engine) = **£54 per car**

Therefore to find the point of MC = MR, we can use the equation:

54 = 80 - 0.4x

0.4x = 26

x = 65

This can now be plugged into our price equation:

P = 80 - 0.2x

P = 67

Therefore, if the Engine division acted to maximise their own profit, the group will sell 65 units at £67 per car, generating revenue of £4,355.

Profit maximisation of the group

To maximise the group's profit, we would simply set the transfer price to the lowest possible price available. In most cases, that is a price equal to **marginal cost**. That way the transferor division suffers no loss (other than opportunity cost, if any), and the transferee division receives goods at the cheapest possible price. Let's see how the revenue would be different under such a system:

We already know that we will be setting the transfer price of the engine at the lowest possible price, that is, marginal cost (£12).

From there we need to calculate the marginal cost of a car.

Marginal cost of engine	£12
Marginal cost of car	£18
Total marginal cost	£30

Using the same equation as before, we know the equation for marginal revenue in the Body division is as follows:

MR = 80 - 0.4x

And we are trying to find the point of MC = MR, therefore:

MC = MR

30 = 80 - 0.4x

0.4x = 50

x = 125

Now that we know our quantity, we need to find our selling price. Earlier we determined our price equation for the Body Division was as follows:

P = 80 – 0.2x

Therefore

P = 80 – (0.2 x 125)

P = 80 – 25

P = 55

Therefore the group will sell 125 units at £55 per car, generating revenue of £6,875.

Conclusion

You will already notice how the revenue differs between the two scenarios. When the transferor aims to maximise profit, the group generates revenue of £4,355. When transfer prices are set to maximise the profit of the group in total, revenue increases to £6,875. This simply demonstrates that when a manager sets transfer prices to maximise his/her division's profit, it will not always provide the best outcome for the organisation as a whole.

The challenge for central management therefore, is to develop a system where both the individual divisions and the group are able to maximise profit.

Opportunity cost based transfer prices

We've already discussed the idea of a minimum and a maximum transfer price; the minimum being marginal cost, and the maximum being market price. No division will transfer their product at less than marginal cost as they will make a loss, and no division will receive a product at a price above what is available in the market.

One possible transfer pricing system that usually lands somewhere in the middle is one based on opportunity cost. The transferor will sell at marginal cost, plus any contribution foregone in the transfer (such as the profit it loses from not selling to an outside customer).

The below example will demonstrate why this approach is considered to be the most mathematically accurate.

Example:

Let's assume there are 2 divisions in Toy Cars Ltd.

The Engine Division manufactures engines at a marginal cost of £10. The engines sell on the open market for £20.

The Body Division manufactures toy cars, each of which include one engine. The cars are produced at a marginal cost of £6 (excluding the cost of the engine). The market price for a car is £24.

Let's look at two scenarios, one where the engine division has no capacity constraints, and another where capacity is limited.

Scenario A: Unlimited capacity

Body division	Marginal cost	Market price	Opportunity cost
Transfer price	(£10)	(£20)	(£10)
Marginal cost	(£6)	(£6)	(£6)
Selling price	£24	£24	£24
Contribution	£8	(£2)	£8

The first column shows a transfer price based on marginal cost. In this case, the price of manufacturing a car is £16 (£10 transfer price for the engine plus £6 to finish the car). At a selling price of £24, this leads to an £8 contribution to Toy Cars Ltd.

The second column shows a transfer price based on market price. In this case, the price of manufacturing a car is £26 (£20 transfer price for the engine plus £6 to finish the car). At a selling price of £24, this leads to a £2 loss for Toy Cars Ltd.

The third column shows a transfer price based on opportunity cost. Because capacity is unlimited and no sales were foregone, the opportunity cost is the same as marginal cost. In this case, the price of manufacturing a car is £16 (£10 transfer price for the engine plus £6 to finish the car). At a selling price of £24, this leads to an £8 contribution to Toy Cars Ltd.

In this scenario, both marginal cost and opportunity cost based transfer pricing lead to the correct result – a positive contribution which will lead to the Body Division producing and selling the product. Under a market price based system, the manager of the body division would not produce the cars as it causes his division to make a loss, even though it is profitable for the company as a whole. Therefore, a market price based transfer price provides an undesirable result and should not be used.

Scenario B: Limited capacity

Body division	Marginal cost	Market price	Opportunity cost
Transfer price	(£10)	(£20)	(£20)
Marginal cost	(£6)	(£6)	(£6)
Selling price	£24	£24	£24
Contribution	£8	(£2)	(£2)

In this scenario only the final column has changed. The opportunity cost to the Engine Division is no longer just marginal cost. It now consists of the contribution foregone from not selling externally at market price (£10), as well as marginal cost (£10), which totals £20.

This is because capacity is limited. By selling to the Body Division a sale to an external party is lost; the Engine division does not have the ability to sell to both.

In this scenario the correct decision would be for the Body Division not to manufacture the cars, as this would result in an overall loss for Toy Cars Ltd. This is because the engine division can achieve a higher contribution from simply selling the engines externally (£10). This is in comparison to the £8 contribution the company receives when the Body Division sells a finished car.

You may have already noticed that the opportunity cost based transfer pricing system is the only one that returns the correct result in both scenarios.

Why is this?

First off, it takes into account the issue of capacity. This ensures that the transferor division does not suffer any loss as a result of the internal transfer. The transferor is never left in a worse off position than if he had sold externally, and the transferee receives a price that is cheaper than market. This satisfies the first requirement of a good transfer pricing system, which is **equity**.

Secondly, using opportunity cost ensures that the system is **neutral**. The transferor receives the same amount whether the unit is sold internally or externally, meaning no profits will be lost by the company as a whole.

While the system works on most levels, it does have the problem of being difficult to implement. In addition to start up issues, opportunity cost in itself can be difficult to quantify, particularly when capacity and market prices fluctuate (which they often do). For these reasons it is often considered a complicated and expensive transfer pricing system.

7. Other considerations in transfer pricing

It is common business practice for international companies to move goods and services between its subsidiaries. While the usual issues with transfer pricing remain relevant here, there is also a new collection of issues that need to be considered.

By setting transfer prices artificially high (or low), multinational organisations have the ability to manipulate profits and taxes in their overseas subsidiaries. This gives them the ability to repatriate profits between countries, minimise payments to shareholders and 'plan' their overseas profits for the most favourable tax outcome. These issues are discussed below:

Taxation

Taxation is considered one of, if not the, main issue with transfer pricing. Many large corporations operate subsidiaries in various countries, which presents the opportunity to manipulate transfer prices in order to minimise taxes. For example, if the tax rate in Hong Kong is lower than the UK, an organisation could simply 'sell' products at an extremely low price to the Hong Kong subsidiary. This would effectively reduce profits in the UK and increase profits in Hong Kong, where the tax rate is significantly lower.

A few years ago in the UK, American coffee house Starbucks were exposed for not paying UK taxes, taxes they had been avoiding by paying inflated rates on coffee beans from the Switzerland subsidiary and by paying excessive 'royalties' to the Dutch subsidiary. In effect hiding costs from other countries in the UK and hiding UK profits elsewhere, making it look like the UK was not making any profit and thus not needing to pay tax.

Taxation authorities now prohibit transfer price fixing in most jurisdictions, and unrealistically high or low transfer prices are often punished with double taxation (tax in both countries). The OECD has since produced guidelines for setting international transfer prices.

The 'arm's length' principle

Today, the accepted practice is that transfer prices should be set at an 'arm's length', meaning the price should be representative of the price that would be agreed upon between two completely unrelated parties.

The most commonly used method of arriving at this price is the **comparable price method**. This involves setting an arm's length transfer price based on comparable products in the market. If this is not possible, a transfer price can be based on gross profit margins in comparable organisations. Again, this is not always possible or accurate, especially when dealing with things such as trademarks and intellectual property. In any case, the onus is on the taxpayer to prove that the transfer price is true and reasonable.

Advanced Pricing Agreements

Because of the uncertainty that can arise in such situations, taxpayers are now able to enter into an Advanced Pricing Agreement (APA) with the relevant tax authorities of the countries involved. This allows the taxpayer to have their transfer prices set in advance, so that any disputes, uncertainty, and risk of penalties are avoided.

Repatriation of funds

When a subsidiary exists overseas, exchange controls can limit the amount of funds that can be repatriated back to the organisation's home country. This is a particularly important issue in times of high inflation, as funds that stay dormant in the host country lose value, whereas the value could be preserved if funds were immediately converted back to the organisation's home currency.

To circumvent these controls, organisations could utilise high transfer prices, so that profits were smaller in the overseas subsidiary and funds would be repatriated via the higher prices being paid.

An example might be if a UK company is doing business in India, where inflation is high. It would be in their best interests to repatriate Indian profits back to the UK as soon as possible to avoid the value of the funds being eroded. If however, some sort of exchange control exists which limits the funds that can be repatriated, the UK company could simply increase transfer prices. The Indian company would then pay funds back to the UK parent in the form of high transfer prices, allowing the company to bring funds back to the UK and preserve the value of their profits.

The opposite of this is if import duty and taxes are high. In that case, it is beneficial to keep transfer prices as low as possible in order to minimise the duty that needs to be paid between transfers.

Minority shareholders

As we've seen, artificially high transfer prices can be used to significantly reduce a subsidiary's profit. An organisation can therefore reduce the payouts required to any minority shareholders in the subsidiaries simply by setting transfer prices in a way that minimises profit.

8. Transfer pricing summary

The issue of transfer pricing arises in decentralised organisations, where the company has various strategic business units operating autonomously. When goods are transferred between the divisions, a 'transfer price' needs to be set. Cost based transfer prices often lead to dysfunctional behaviour, as supplying divisions do not realise a profit and therefore lack motivation. Market based transfer prices can lead to divisions buying goods externally that can be produced cheaper in-house. Therefore, the decision on whether prices are set based on market price, marginal cost, absorption cost or opportunity cost is a decision that central management must make based on their own goals and strategy. Mathematically, a price based on marginal cost plus opportunity cost offers the most mathematically sound result.

Aside from internal considerations, transfer pricing also gives rise to issues such as tax manipulation and repatriation of overseas funds. There are now laws surrounding this and one should be aware of the need to set 'arm's length' transfer prices and the option of entering into Advanced Price Agreements.

CIMA P3 Course Notes

Chapter 7
Controlling Information Systems

1. The importance of IT

Information Technology (IT) is a key part of almost any organisation's success in the modern age. Every internal department needs and effective system to be efficient while customer facing systems, such as a company's website are becoming increasingly important to a company's success.

IT must therefore be well managed and controlled and that's the subject of this chapter.

2. Information strategies

Information strategies are plans for how information and the company's information systems will contribute to the organisations success in the future. They include plans for specific IT systems, how they are developed and managed.

Reasons to have an information strategy

Having a formal, documented, planned IS strategy is important for the following reasons:

- Opportunity to gain **competitive advantage** (e.g. to improve the quality of products or service provided)

- **Focused IT expenditure** (which can be very high so it's important spending is in the right place)

- **IT is critical to some organisations** (e.g. Google, Microsoft, Amazon) and an inherent part of their product and service and so must be well planned and organised

- Opportunity to **reduce costs** and gain efficiencies

- **Many stakeholders** are affected as IT is used throughout the organisation and beyond (e.g. by customers) and it's relevant to all stakeholders and so must be planned

- New **systems take a long time to develop** so need long term planning

- **Rapid changes in IT** with constant opportunities and threats means ongoing planning is needed

- **Compatibility** of systems throughout the organisation.

From a control perspective it enables much greater control of information systems (IS) throughout the organisation and so a plan (or strategy(is an important control system.

Aligning information strategies with the business strategy

The **information strategies must be aligned with the business strategy** to ensure that it is consistent with the over-riding direction of the organisation and that IT as a whole is used in a way that benefits the business in the best way. For example, a company whose strategic focus is based around quality, should invest in information systems which help support the production of high quality products and good service.

Information strategies

There are three types of information strategies:

a)   Information systems (IS) strategy

b)   Information technology (IT) strategy

c)   Information management (IM) strategy

Information systems (IS) strategy

The Information Systems (IS) Strategy sets out to provide a long term direction for the development of information systems throughout the organisation.

It can include:

- a statement of corporate goals.

- how the organisation aims to use information and information technology to support those goals(e.g. to gain competitive advantage, to keep costs low, to provide customer service).

- the key information requirements (from CSFs).

- the principles which guide the acquisition, development and replacement of information systems;

- the current priorities for system acquisition, modification.

- target objectives and milestones that can be used to judge progress.

Information technology (IT) strategy

The information technology strategy is concerned with the development and maintenance of hardware and software to facilitate the overall IS strategy (e.g. to provide the required information).

Information management (IM) strategy

The information management (IM) strategy outlines how the organisation will control and manage information in the organisation. It includes:

a) IT function
 - size
 - responsibilities
 - centralised or decentralised IT decision making

b) Financial control
 - Investment appraisal criteria
 - Approach to budgeting and monitoring of IT budgets
 - Performance measurement of IT projects

c) Technology development
 - Approach to security
 - Systems development methodologies to be used

d) Planning

- Integration of IT/IS with other departments

3. Managing the IS department

For full control of all aspects of information systems in an organisation a well organised, managed and staffed IS department is crucial.

Responsibilities of the IS Department can include:

- Defining the IS/IT/IM strategies
- User support (information centres) and training
- Systems development
- Defining hardware and software standards
- Systems security
- IT purchasing
- To liaise with other parts of the organisation to ensure their IS needs are being met

- Systems maintenance
- Control of network (e.g. hardware and software upgrades, updating software)
- Data processing
- Database administration

4. Steering committee

The steering committee provides a high level management role over IS development and practise for the organisation and as such are a key organisational control mechanism.

As well as IS department members the steering committee also includes senior members of the different departments within the organisation to ensure that IS strategy and systems developed reflect the broad organisational needs.

Responsibilities of the steering committee include:

- Aligning IS/IT strategy with organisational strategy
- Allocating resources to specific IS projects in accordance with the strategy
- Creating objectives for development projects
- Monitoring progress of development projects.

5. Big data

Big data and it's uses

Big data is a term used to describe sets of data so large that they simply cannot be analysed and interpreted by standard reporting facilities. The value of big data is that it allows you to draw from an enormous amount of different data as opposed to having many separate sets. As a result it can be possible to identify unusual business trends and correlations that would otherwise be impossible to spot.

Big data has the potential for almost universal application; here are some examples of big data being implemented in the real world:

- Used by some hospitals to monitor patient details and the treatment sought, meaning they can assess the likelihood of readmission and if high make sure the issue is resolved there and then thus saving time and money further down the line.

- Consumer goods companies monitoring facebook/twitter and as a result gaining key and an uninhibited insight into consumer behaviour which they then use in their marketing campaigns.

- Governments can use them to measure crime rates as big data allows the inclusion of many other factors which in theory can help determine why crime rates are increasing/decreasing rather than just the fact that they are.

Gartner's Three Vs

In a 2001 research report **Gartner** outlined three key challenges faces organisations with their data. These three elements are:

Volume - increasing volumes of data mean there is a lot more to manage and it is harder to extract key information from it

Velocity – there is an increasing speed of data in and out, which means data can quickly change. This means that information analysis needs to be quick to spot and react to the latest change.

Variety – the range of data types and sources of data can be varied making analysis difficult. e.g. data in different IT systems in an organisation being hard to bring together to analyse linkages.

Gartner then came up with a formal definition of big data related to these 3Vs which is:

Big data is high volume, high velocity, and/or high variety information assets that require new forms of processing to enable enhanced decision making, insight discovery and process optimisation.

The seven stages of the big data process

The seven key stages and challenges that make up the big data process are as follows:

Capture – What kind of data is needed and how is going to be captured. This is usually an indirect source (rather than manual data input), a prime example would be the barcode reader in a retail outlet.

Storage – As you might expect, the amount of data we are talking about cannot be simply saved on a laptop hard drive. Big data sets can require physical systems that take up entire rooms or even buildings. In addition to the sheer size needed both physically and memory-wise you will need to make sure the systems are adequately protected as you may have access to private customer information.

Curation – Once the data has been captured it then must be organised, controlled after and maintained in a way that allows it to be usable and re-usable, an on-going, day to day upkeep of the data in effect. This may involve the way it is structured on the system to enable it to be analysed.

Analysis - The process of interpreting the data, millions of bits of info means nothing unless you can use to help answer questions/illustrate results etc. This could be the ability to separate the data out by date, product, customer or make linkages between different types of data e.g. sales made by customer group at different times of the year.

Visualisation - The data which is analysed needs to be illustrated in a clear and digestible format so that it can be used to make decisions. This may take the form of graphs or condensed simple tables.

Search - When you have as much data as a big data system can compile you must find a way to search across the vast data landscape to find the info you want. An example of a search system would be google; which can accurately search through billions of web pages based on a few key search terms. Each 'big data' system needs it's own 'google' type search system to access the relevant data and help users access relevant information.

Data Sharing and Transfer - Data must be shared with those who need it so that relevant people can access the information produced and indeed relevant information is proactively sent to the people who can best use the information gained.

Big data as a strategic resource

Big data is increasingly becoming of strategic importance. As an example, retailers that understand their customers and their needs better by analysing big data are able to produce better products, target marketing campaigns better and price products in a way that attracts more custom based on past buying patterns. Together this can provide firms who use Big Data effectively a competitive advantage.

6. Systems development

One key aspect of IS control involves detailed control over the development of new systems by following a standardised step by step model of clear discreet stages. These stages are outlined in the systems development life cycle.

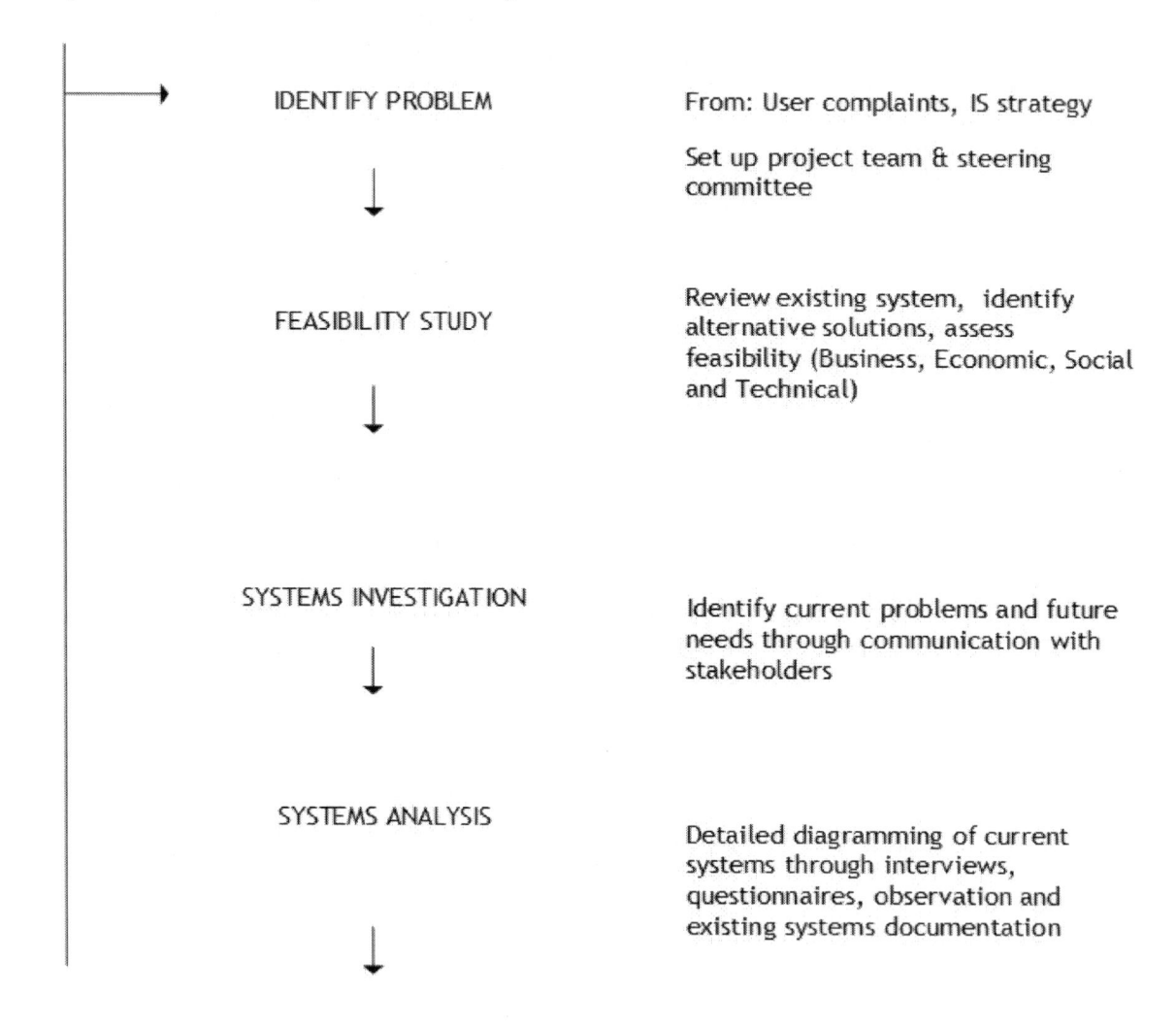

Systems development lifecycle

IDENTIFY PROBLEM — From: User complaints, IS strategy. Set up project team & steering committee

↓

FEASIBILITY STUDY — Review existing system, identify alternative solutions, assess feasibility (Business, Economic, Social and Technical)

↓

SYSTEMS INVESTIGATION — Identify current problems and future needs through communication with stakeholders

↓

SYSTEMS ANALYSIS — Detailed diagramming of current systems through interviews, questionnaires, observation and existing systems documentation

↓

SYSTEMS DESIGN

Design of new system - Processes, External design (screen designs, output and input methods), Security.

↓

PROGRAMMING AND TESTING

Write/buy software.

Selection of hardware.

↓

Testing (program & integration).

IMPLEMENTATION

File conversion

Install hardware and software

↓

User training

SYSTEMS REVIEW AND MAINTENANCE

Review systems performance

Maintenance: Corrective, Adaptive and Perfective

Benefits for a formal systems development methodology based on the systems development lifecycle include:

- Considers all key elements of systems development
- Sign off of each stage - ensures completeness, appropriateness, meets needs.
- Clearly documented process - aids subsequent development and updating
- Users involved at early stages
- Good diagramming techniques used - aids understanding of system
- Clear project management and control

7. IT controls

Up until now we've considered strategic level control of IT - strategies and IT development. Both are crucial. However in the modern age one of the most important elements of controlling organisations are those controls built into the day to day operation of IT systems. As a simple example in financial systems modern systems will only allow correct double entry, will automatically balance the balance sheet, ensure the sales ledger and general ledger always balance, spot and disallow some input errors and so on.

There are a number of different categories of IT controls which we'll look at one by one:

Physical controls

Physical controls concern the environment in which the system is kept. These include physical controls to prevent:

Fire damage - fire alarms, sprinkler systems, extinguishers to hand

Flood damage - Avoid sitting systems in basements or other vulnerable areas, building maintenance to avoid leeks

Power failure - Back up generators, current isolators (to minimise damage through electricity fluctuations)

Unauthorised access - locks on doors, security guards

Theft - Locked computers, alarms, disks kept in locked cabinet.

Administrative controls

Administrative controls are formalised standards, rules, and procedures on the use of systems. They ensure the security of systems through the rules and procedures imposed on people using the system. For example this might include rules or procedures on:

- Checking data input against control totals
- Authorisation of transactions before processing
- Authorisation of system changes
- Regular back-ups undertaken

Administrative controls include:

Passwords

A password is a number or set of characters (or a mixture of the two) which must be entered into a system to allow access.

Passwords are an essential way to prevent unauthorised access to data.

Passwords should be:

- Changed regularly
- Not written down
- Not given to other people
- Not associated to something familiar to the user

A back up system to allow people to access or change forgotten passwords must be available to ensure people can continue use the system without delay.

Encryption

Encryption is used to ensure that documents can not be accessed by unauthorised users. When a document is encrypted it is converted into a secret code which only the intended recipient can decipher.

Encryption is commonly used when sending documents using public telephone lines e.g. when using the internet to pay using credit cards.

Anti-virus software

Computer viruses are small programs which attach themselves to files in a computer. They replicate themselves onto other computers which access these files and can thus spread from computer to computer. Many modern viruses make use of flaws in e-mail software to automatically send themselves out to everyone on the individual's address book.

Viruses are written by unscrupulous individuals largely for the fun of it. The consequences of viruses can be varied, from no effect to the entire contents of the hard-drive being erased.

To prevent viruses an organisation can use virus checking software. These identify and help to remove viruses found on the system. They automatically check incoming e-mails and downloaded files for viruses.

Application controls

IT application or program controls are fully automated (i.e. performed automatically by the systems) and designed to ensure the complete and accurate processing of data, from input through output. These controls vary based on the business purpose of the specific application. These controls may also help ensure the privacy and security of data transmitted between applications. Categories of IT application controls may include:

Completeness checks - controls that ensure all records were processed from initiation to completion.

Validity checks - controls that ensure only valid data is input or processed.

Identification - controls that ensure all users are uniquely identified (e.g. to ensure only the correct owner of a bank account has access through use of multiple passwords)

Authorisation - controls that ensure only approved users can undertake certain tasks.

Forensic controls - control that ensure data is scientifically correct and mathematically correct based on inputs and outputs. e.g. the balance sheet balances.

Contingency controls – disaster recovery

A contingency plan outlines the steps which will be taken in case of a 'disaster' such as a fire, flood, damage caused by a virus, theft of important systems. This is vital since many organisations are dependent upon systems. The longer the system is down the worse the consequences.

Disaster recovery plans can include:

- Creation of processing facilities on separate sites
- Agreements with other company's to share systems in times of disaster.
- Computer bureaux
- Back-up systems

Audit trail

An audit trail is the ability to follow a transaction all the way through a process. Systems should be developed such that a complete audit trail can be followed. Information about the transaction will also be recorded for information purposes (e.g. who made the transaction, when, at what location and so on). This is of use in:

- Testing
- Investigations (e.g. investigating frauds)
- Examining the effectiveness of controls (usually by internal audit)

… astranti
financial training

CIMA P3 Course Notes

Chapter 8
Internal Auditing

1. Internal auditing

What is internal auditing?

Organisations are faced with many risks, and to manage those risks controls are put in place to manage them. However do those controls adequately cover the risks, and are the controls that are in place actually being applied as they should be? If not then the control system will not work. It makes sense then to have a team in the organisation who are responsible for the review of processes and controls and to advise on how to improve them. That's the main role of internal audit.

Now internal audit also do other things too, and can take on a broader role reviewing on and advising the business and so we have a broader definition of their role which is as follows:

Internal auditing is an independent, objective assurance and consulting activity designed to add value and improve an organisation's operations.

Purpose of internal auditing

If we were to sum up the over=riding purpose of internal controls then we might say that it helps an organisation accomplish its objectives by bringing a systematic, disciplined approach to evaluate and improve **the effectiveness of risk management, control, and governance processes**.

Internal auditing aims to help in improving an organisation's effectiveness and efficiency by providing recommendations on how to improve the **efficiency and effectiveness of the organisation** and its procedures and controls.

With commitment to integrity and accountability, internal auditing provides value to governing bodies and senior management as an **objective source of independent advice**.

Scope of internal audit

The scope of internal auditing within an organisation is broad and may involve topics such as the efficacy of operations, the reliability of financial reporting, deterring and investigating fraud, safeguarding assets, and compliance with laws and regulations.

Compliance audits - Internal auditing most frequently involves measuring compliance with the entity's policies and procedures, by identifying procedures and controls, testing these and reporting on how well they are applied and how they might be improved. These may also be used to identify occurrence of fraud.

Other types of auditing include:

Value for money auditing – Auditor's investigate the **E**ffectiveness, **E**fficiency and **E**conomy of a department or division and recommend improvements. This is common in the public sector where there is no profit motive to drive the 3E's.

Management audits – These review the performance of managers and their divisions and suggest improvements in performance.

Social and environmental audits – These focus on Corporate Social Responsibility and environmental issues and the organisation's performance in these areas, alongside compliance with internal policies and external regulation.

Fraud investigations – Where fraud is identified (e.g. as part of a systems audit) specific investigation of the frauds may be undertaken to identify the cause and extent. Information may be used to support a legal case, and recommendations will be made to avoid similar frauds in the future.

Post-implementation project reviews/audits – At the end of major projects, the final step is to review the effectiveness of the project and learn lessons to apply to future projects. While often this is carried out by the project manager, sometimes the internal audit team take part in this review as it helps bring independence to the assessment.

Role in risk management

Internal auditors monitor and evaluate the effectiveness of the organisation's risk management processes and they support the Board and Audit committee in their work understanding and managing risk.

Internal auditors may help companies establish and maintain Enterprise Risk Management processes. In the US, internal auditors also play an important role in helping companies execute top-down risk assessments required under Sarbanes-Oxley corporate governance regulations. In these latter two areas, internal auditors typically are part of the risk assessment team in an advisory role.

2. Developing the audit plans

Plan of audit engagements

Internal auditing standards require the development of a plan of audit engagements based on a risk assessment, updated at least annually. The input of senior management and the Board (often through the Audit Committee) is typically included in this process. Many departments update their plan of engagements throughout the year as risks or organisational priorities change. This ensures the audit activity is aligned with the organisation's strategic and operational objectives.

Internal auditors often conduct a series of interviews of senior management to identify potential audit engagements. If the organisation has a formal enterprise risk management (ERM) program, the risks identified therein help will guide the work of the internal audit department.

The preliminary plan of engagements is documented and prioritised. Audit resources and expertise are then considered and a final plan is presented to senior management and the Audit Committee.

Plan for each audit

Each audit will need to be planned and organised considering issues such as:

- skills required (e.g. are their complex transactions than need a specialist to review and analyse)
- team members
- timing and duration (i.e. convenient both for the audit team and the department being audited)
- key risks
- the nature of the audit tests to be undertaken (e.g. detailed testing analytical review – see later)
- other resources required

Audit risk

One key element of planning the audit is understanding the audit risk.

Audit risk refers to the risk that an auditor may fail to detect material errors, problems or misstatement of accounting balances.

This risk is composed of inherent risk (IR), control risk (CR) and detection risk (DR), and can be calculated thus:

$$AR = IR \times CR \times DR$$

IR is inherent risk – the risk inherent in the issue (e.g. there is a high inherent risk of theft of cash from a bank, and a low inherent risk of theft of the bank's marketing banner – significant controls should be in place over theft of of cash, but not the marketing banner therefore)

CR is control risk - the risk that a misstatement or error could occur but may not be detected and corrected or prevented by entity's internal control mechanism. The key question here is – how good are the current controls? Are they sufficient and adequate?

DR is detection risk - this is probability that the audit procedures may fail to detect existence of a material error or fraud. For instance, audit tests may find it harder to find errors in highly complex transactions (e.g. futures and options), than straightforward ones such as a purchase.

The audit will tend to plan to review areas where the Inherent Risk is high as these are key threats. Where the control risk is low, as there are good controls in place then the audit will primarily be involved in testing these controls rather than advising on new ones. Where detection risk is high, then there needs to be more testing or special audit procedures put in place.

3. Undertaking an internal audit

Steps in internal audits

Internal auditing activity is generally conducted as one or more discrete assignments. A typical internal audit assignment involves the following steps:

- Establish and communicate the **scope and objectives** for the audit to appropriate management.

- Develop an **understanding of the business area under review**. This includes objectives, processes, and key transaction types. This involves review of documents and interviews. Flowcharts are commonly used to map processes.

- Describe the **key risks** facing the business activities within the scope of the audit.

- **Identify existing control procedures** used to ensure each key risk and transaction type is properly controlled and monitored. These may be identified using **internal control questionnaires** given to key staff working on the process to identify how the processes work.

- Develop and execute a **risk-based sampling and testing** approach to **determine whether the most important controls are operating as intended**. Samples are chosen at random and must represent a true view of the population being tested to ensure the test is fair and representative.

- **Report problems** identified.

- Negotiate **action plans** with management to address the problems.

- **Follow-up** on reported findings at appropriate intervals. Internal audit departments maintain a follow-up database for this purpose.

Audit assignment length varies based on the complexity of the activity being audited and Internal Audit resources available.

4. Analytical review

Analytical review

Analytical procedures are one of many financial audit processes which help an auditor understand the business and changes in the business, and to identify potential risk areas to plan other audit procedures.

Analytical procedures include comparison of financial information (data in financial statement) with

- prior periods
- budgets
- forecasts
- data on similar companies/industries

It also includes consideration of predictable relationships (or ratios), such as:

- gross profit to sales,
- payroll costs to employees,
- financial information and non-financial information, for examples the CEO's reports and the industry news.

These comparisons are used to identify unusual items in the test which can then be investigated further to identify whether the unexpected variation is valid.

Unusual or unexpected items can then be investigated to find the underlying causes, and where a problem is found this reported and action taken.

Let's look at the performance of the following hotels in a group of hotels:

Hotel	Budget profit	Actual profit
London	700,000	300,000
Paris	600,000	600,000
Berlin	400,000	400,000
New York	200,000	-100,000
Singapore	900,000	900,000
Moscow	100,000	100,000
Colombo	400,000	800,000
Sydney	300,000	300,000
Mumbai	200,000	200,000

You'll notice here that most hotels have hit their targets, and these are less of a concern for the auditors. However, the auditors might investigate London and New York in particular to find out what the reasons for the lower than expected profits are to make sure that there are not errors, frauds or management or control problems.

This is example is very high level, and in reality auditors tend to test smaller elements of a business, and so are more likely to be looking at a more specific comparison, so for example when reviewing inventory within the business they might compare data such as the inventory days (inventory/purchases x 365) to test inventory balances.

Hotel	Inventory days
London	17
Paris	17
Berlin	14
New York	20
Singapore	56
Moscow	7
Colombo	8
Sydney	19
Mumbai	16

In this case the auditors might wonder why inventory days are so much lower than average in Colombo and Moscow and so much higher than average in Singapore. Is that indicative of a problem or issue (e.g. theft of stock) or simply related to the nature of the business in different markets? The Singapore hotel could, for instance, have a shop attached to it which would naturally mean it would have higher inventory days than a hotel. Alternatively it could just be poor management or processing errors.

Benchmarking

Benchmarking is formally defined as the comparison of performance and business processes to the best in the industry or best practices from other industries, with the aim of learning from those practises to improve performance in the future.

Benchmarking can involve different types of performance comparison including with:

- Other organisations in the same industry (**external or competitive benchmarking**)
- a business function or process(e.g. finance) with similar divisions of other (usually non-competing) organisations (**functional or process benchmarking**)

- similar divisions within the organisation itself e.g. two similar retail outlets **(internal benchmarking)**.

Benchmarking and the internal auditor

When undertaking analytical reviews the auditor is effectively comparing performance of the division or organisation as a whole against budget, other departments or other organisations to look for unusual patterns or activities. The focus is usually to identify unusual transactions - things that are different from what we might expect to find errors or problems.

However, the remit of internal audits is not just to find errors or problems but to suggest improvements in business processes. As such benchmarking can be a useful tool as part of the audit process. If we are to return to our hotels example we might notice that the profits in Colombo are much higher than budget, and inventory days lower than average. This looks like a very well performing hotel - the internal audit what can be learnt from this and shared with other hotels in the group?

What are the difficulties when benchmarking?

A key difficulty with benchmarking is how to successfully get relevant **information about competitor performance**. Financial performance may be able to be obtained through company accounts, the company's product can be purchased to trial and test it, but ultimately a competitor is unlikely to exchange important information about internal processes and results. Functional benchmarking can overcome this problem by exchanging information with non-competing organisations.

In addition, even where information is available, for instance in company accounts, it can be hard to make **meaningful and fair comparisons** due to differences in the businesses or business process, and so data needs to be very carefully analysed.

5. Computer-assisted audit techniques

Auditing in a computer environment

Auditing in a computer environment can be difficult due to the lack of an audit trail through a computer system, and a lack of physical evidence of controls having been applied. The sheer volume of transactions can also make auditing difficult due to the amount of work required.

CAATS

Computer-assisted audit techniques or computer-assisted audit techniques (CAATS) is the practice of using computers to automate the audit process.

One example is using computers in audits is **Audit Interrogation Software** to examine groups of transactions. The software can extract every transaction the business unit performed during the period reviewed. The auditor will then test that data to determine if there are any problems in the data. This improves on traditional auditing which would only test a sample.

For example, the auditor could quickly identify duplicate invoices or transactions. When such a duplicate is identified, they can approach management with the knowledge that they tested 100% of the transactions and that they identified 100% of the exceptions.

However, the CAATS driven review is limited only to the data saved on files in accordance with a systematic pattern. Much data is never documented this way. In addition saved data often contains deficiencies, is poorly classified, is not easy to get, and it might be hard to become convinced about its integrity.

6. Internal audit reports

Internal auditors typically issue reports at the end of each audit that summarise their findings, recommendations, and any responses or action plans from management. An audit report may have:

- an executive summary

- a body that includes the specific issues or findings identified and related recommendations or action plans

- an appendix with information such as detailed graphs and charts or process.

Each audit finding within the body of the report may contain five elements, sometimes called the "5 Cs":

Condition: What is the particular problem identified?

Criteria: What is the standard that was not met? The standard may be a company policy or other benchmark.

Cause: Why did the problem occur?

Consequence: What is the risk/negative outcome (or opportunity foregone) because of the finding?

Corrective action: What should management do about the finding? What have they agreed to do and by when?

The recommendations in an internal audit report are designed to help the organisation achieve its goals, which may relate to operations, financial reporting or legal/regulatory compliance.

7. Effective internal audit

Organisational independence

To perform their role effectively, internal auditors require organisational independence from management, to enable unrestricted evaluation of management activities and personnel.

Although internal auditors are part of company management and paid by the company, the primary customer of internal audit activity is the entity charged with oversight of management's activities. The internal auditors typically report to the Audit Committee, a sub-committee of the Board of Directors.

In order to be independent:

1) The Head of Internal Audit must report to a level within the organisation that allows the internal audit activity to fulfil its responsibilities (e.g. the Audit committee or Chairman)

2) The internal audit activity must be free from interference in determining the scope of internal auditing, performing work, and communicating results

3) The Head of Internal Audit must communicate and interact directly with the Board of Directors preferably through the Audit Committee.

Auditor ethics

To be effective it is vital that the department acts in and has a reputation for operating with high ethical standards. CIMA's ethical principles can be applied to the work of internal auditors:

Integrity means being straightforward, honest and truthful in all professional and business relationships. All internal audit work must be conducted correctly and honestly.

Objectivity means not allowing bias, conflict of interest or the influence of other people, to override professional judgement. To protect your objectivity, internal auditors should not work for you should avoid working in areas of the business where relationships could bias or overly influence their professional opinion. e.g. if they're auditing work conducted by a friend or family member.

Professional competence and due care is an ongoing commitment to maintain a level of professional knowledge and skill. The internal auditor should have skills in audit and in the items being audited e.g. an account would be the best person to review the finance controls. Updates should be undertaken on current developments in the individual's area of work, legislation and regulation.

Confidentiality means respecting the confidential nature of information acquired. Internal auditors have access to confidential information throughout the organisation and as such it is particularly important for them and the integrity of the department that any confidential information is kept within the team.

Professional behaviour requires individuals to comply with relevant laws and regulations. Internal auditors should follow internal audit standards. Professionals, such as accountants, must also avoid any action that could negatively affect the reputation of their profession.

Other elements of effective internal audit

Other elements of effective internal audit include:

- Adequate numbers of staff
- Sufficiently skilled staff
- Standardised and robust audit procedures
- Authority to be able to investigate whatever they feel is necessary when they feel it is necessary
- Clear leadership
- A remit to review the whole organisation an **'organisational remit'** (as opposed to just finance) so that all key risks can be reviewed and managed as opposed to just those in certain departments.

Measuring the internal audit function

Internal audit functions are primarily evaluated based on the quality of advice and information provided to the Audit Committee and top management. However, this is primarily qualitative and therefore difficult to measure. "Customer surveys" sent to key managers after each audit engagement or report can be used to measure performance, with an annual survey of the Audit Committee.

Scoring on dimensions such as professionalism, quality of counsel, timeliness of work product, utility of meetings, and quality of status updates are typical with such surveys.

Understanding the expectations of senior management and the audit committee represent important steps in developing a performance measurement process, as well as how such measures help align the audit function with organisational priorities.

Quantitative measures can also be used to measure the function's level of execution and qualifications of its personnel. Key measures include:

Plan completion: This is a measure of the degree to which the annual plan of engagements are completed.

Report issuance: This is a measure of the time elapsed from completion of testing to issuance of the final audit report, including management's action plans.

Issue closure: Reported audit findings are often called "issues" or "deficiencies." Professional standards require audit functions to track reported findings to resolution, which effectively requires the maintenance of an issues follow-up database.

Staff qualifications: This can be measured through the percentage of staff with professional certifications, graduate degrees, and overall years of experience.

Staff utilisation rate: This is measured as the percentage of time spent on audit engagements, as opposed to administrative time such as training or holiday.

Staffing level: The number of positions filled relative to the authorised staffing level.

8. Role in corporate governance

The internal auditor is often considered one of the "four pillars" of corporate governance, the other pillars being the Board of Directors, management, and the external auditor.

A primary focus area of internal auditing as it relates to corporate governance is **helping the Audit Committee perform its responsibilities effectively**. This may include reporting critical internal control problems, informing the Committee privately on the capabilities of key managers, suggesting questions or topics for the Audit Committee's meeting agendas, and coordinating carefully with the external auditor and management to ensure the Committee receives effective information.

The Head of Internal Audit typically reports the most critical issues to the Audit Committee quarterly, along with management's progress towards resolving them.

Critical issues typically have a reasonable likelihood of causing substantial financial or reputational damage to the company.

9. Relationship with the external auditor

What is an external auditor?

The external auditor is an independent firm engaged by the client subject to the audit, to express an opinion on whether the company's financial statements are free of material misstatements, whether due to fraud or error.

In the US, under Sarbanes Oxley for publicly-traded companies, external auditors are also required to express an opinion over the effectiveness of internal controls over financial reporting.

Comparison with internal audit

The remit of internal auditors is much wider than external auditors. Internal auditors are focused on the whole organisation and its controls and processes, while external auditors focus on the financial statements.

Internal auditors report to, and are responsible to management while external auditors are responsible to shareholders.

Relationship between internal and external auditors

External auditors may rely on work done by internal auditors as part of the evidence they build as part of their external audit work, and the type and timing of the work of internal auditors may be planned to help support the external audit.

CIMA P3 Course Notes

Chapter 9

Financial Risk

1. What is financial risk?

Definition

Financial risks relate to:

- financing the business (such as changing interest rates or non-availability of finance)
- undertaking financial transactions (such as exchange rate risk or non-payment by a customer)
- the possibility that an investment's actual return will be different than expected. This includes the possibility of losing some or all of the original investment.

Due to the nature of financial risk they are often among the most significant risks in any organisation, and as such are a key focus for the audit committee, risk committee, risk manager and internal audit department.

As management accountants we must be clearly aware of these risks and actively ensure these are managed and controlled within the organisation.

2. Investment risks

These are risks related to investments in shares, loans, and other securities.

Market risk

This is the risk that the value of a portfolio, either an investment portfolio or a trading portfolio, will decrease due to the change in market risk factors. The four standard market risk factors are as follows:

Equity risk is the risk that stock prices in general (not related to a particular company or industry) will change or become more volatile.

Interest rate risk is the risk that interest rates will change or become more volatile.

Currency risk is the risk that foreign exchange rates or the implied volatility will change, which affects, for example, the value of an asset held in that currency.

Commodity risk is the risk that commodity prices (e.g. corn, copper, crude oil) or implied volatility will change.

Asset-backed risk

Asset backed risk is the risk that the changes in assets supported by an asset-backed security will significantly impact the value of the supported security. For example, a mortgage portfolio backed by property assets will fall in value during significant downturns in the property market. Credit risk

Credit risk, also called default risk, is the risk associated with a borrower going into default (not making payments as promised). Investor losses include lost principal and interest, decreased cash flow, and increased collection costs.

Political or Foreign investment risk

Political, or foreign investment risk, is the risk of rapid and extreme changes in value due to political or other changes in a country in which an investment arises. This could be due to effects such as nationalisation of industries, tax changes, or political or diplomatic changes.

Liquidity risk (of investments)

This is the risk that a given security or asset cannot be traded quickly enough in the market to prevent a loss (or make the required profit). Private sector shares can have significant liquidity risk as it may take many months or years to find a buyer, agree a price and make a sale.

Currency risk

This is the changing value of investments due to currency movements of overseas investments.

3. Financial risks associated with international operations

When operating overseas companies face an increased number of financial risks that do not apply to operations in the home country. Let's look at a number of these.

Currency risk

Currency risk is the potential change in the exchange rate of one currency against another. Investors or businesses face an exchange rate risk when they have assets or operations across national borders or if they have loans or borrowings in a foreign currency.

An exchange rate risk can result in an exchange gain as well as a loss. Great concern occurs when there is possibility that currency depreciation will negatively affect the value of one's assets, investments, and their related interest and dividend payment streams, especially those securities denominated in foreign currency.

There are two key types of currency risk

Transaction risk

Transaction risk is the risk that an exchange rate will change unfavourably over time. It is **associated with the time delay between entering into a contract and settling it**. The greater the time differential between the entrance and settlement of the contract, the greater the transaction risk, because there is more time for the two exchange rates to fluctuate.

Transaction risk can be managed using hedging techniques – see later.

Translation risk

Translation risk is an accounting concept. It is proportional to the amount of assets held in foreign currencies. Changes in the exchange rate over time will change the value of assets when converted back into the business' home currency when reporting in the financial statements. The whole balance sheet value could deteriorate in the home currency despite the overseas operations actually being more successful – it's just that the exchange rate has changed.

These risks are usually mitigated by netting assets in that currency with by borrowings in that currency, hence reducing the net value to be translated into the home currency for financial reporting purposes.

Political risk

Political and legal change and uncertainty can affect the profitability of markets, taxes and tariff's paid and the exchange and interest rates payable on loans.

Changing political circumstances and law can be monitored and contingency plans drawn up. It may also help to:

- Build relationships with governments and gain their support or finance
- Work in joint ventures with local companies
- Obtain local finance, and be seen to be investing in the local economy.
- Diversify the business in many different markets to avoid over-dependence on any single market.

Economic risk

Changing economic positions in countries in which the business operates or with whom they trade affects interest rates, exchange rates and the general market conditions affecting profitability.

Economic conditions in overseas markets can be monitored and remedial action taken as necessary (e.g. pulling out of unprofitable markets). Diversification in many different markets can also avoid over dependence on a single economy.

4. Quantifying risk

Unlike many other risks, as financial risk is monetarily related it also means that financial risks can be clearly evaluated. We can relate this back to the risk management steps, and the assessment of impact. With financial risks often the 'impact' can be properly evaluated. Let's look at some methods.

Expected values

An expected value of risk is the long run average loss that will be expected over a period of time.

Expected value = probability of loss over set time frame x value of loss

For example, if there was a 1% chance of a fire in the next year causing a £1m loss, the expected value is £10,000.

This value might then be compared against the cost of insurance to decide whether to take it our or simply accept the risk.

Standard deviation

Standard deviation is a measure of the variability around the mean (or average). The higher the standard deviation the greater the variability and therefore the greater the risk. This might for example be measured for the variability of share or portfolio of shares.

The absolute value of the standard deviation of one item (e.g. one stock) is not directly comparable to that of another (e.g. another stock), so a more comparable measure the **coefficient of variation** can be used by dividing the standard deviation by the mean to get a ratio.

Value at risk (VaR)

Value at risk is a statistical method of measuring risks based on

- Mean – long run average change in the value of the transaction or portfolio
- Standard deviation – Measure of the variability of the returns

The calculation provides the maximum loss that will be experienced given normal market movements for a specific level of certainty

This enables portfolio managers to assess the level of risk taken each day/week/month on a portfolio

For example, if a portfolio of stocks has a one-day 5% VaR of $1 million, there is a 0.05 probability that the portfolio will fall in value by more than $1 million over a one day period. An alternative way of viewing this is that a loss of $1 million or more on this portfolio is expected on 1 day in 20. A loss which exceeds the VaR threshold is termed a "VaR break."

Value at Risk calculation example

Only very basic VaR calculations are required in this exam, and you can follow a step by step approach to doing these as is shown below. Here's an example:

$1m is being received in 1 years time. Past exchange rate movements suggest that based on past movements in exchange rates the mean change in return will be a loss of $0.05m, with a standard deviation of $0.1m. To 95% certainty level, what is the value at risk (the maximum financial loss at this certainty level)?

Step 1: "100% - confidence level in question"= 100% - 95% = 5%

Step 2: Calculate "50% - answer to step 1" = 50% - 5% = 45%

Then express as a decimal : 0.45

Step 3: On the normal distribution tables given in the exam, look at the myriad of numbers given in the main body of the table and find that closest to the number in step 2

In this example the numbers .4495 and .4505 are nearest. Either can be chosen here then, so let's choose .4505

Step 4: Add the number in the far left column (here. 1.6) to the number in the first row (0.05) to get what is called a **Confidence Interval** (here = 1.65)

Step 5: Use the formula

VaR = Mean deviation - (Confidence interval x standard deviation)

    (given in question)   (given in question)

=   -0.05m   - (1.96   x   0.1   )

=   -0.215m

This means that There is a 95% chance that there will be a loss no greater than $215,000 on this transaction.

5. Diversification

Diversification for investment risk

Diversification is a key way of reducing investment risk. In finance, diversification means reducing risk by investing in a variety of shares, loans or other assets. This has the affect of avoiding exposure to losses on any single investment.

The simplest example of diversification is provided by the proverb "Don't put all your eggs in one basket". Dropping the basket will break all the eggs. Placing each egg in a different basket is more diversified. There is more risk of losing one egg, but less risk of losing all of them.

In finance, an example of an undiversified portfolio is to hold shares in only one company – risking everything on that company which could potentially fail. By holding a portfolio of shares in different companies in different industries means that even if one of those should do poorly it will be balanced against others that do well.

Further diversification can be obtained by investing in stocks from different countries, and in different asset classes such as bonds, property, private equity, infrastructure and commodities such as heating oil or gold. The wider the variety of the investment portfolio the less they depend on each other and the greater the diversification.

Any risk-averse investor will diversify to at least some extent, with more risk-averse investors diversifying more completely than less risk-averse investors which many investors see as an attractive prospect, so that Index Funds have been developed that invest in equities in proportion to the weighting they have in some well known index such as the FTSE.

Diversification does not eliminate the risk that all assets will move in the same direction however. During recessionary times, the whole market for shares tends to fall, so however well an investor is diversified in different types of shares they will still experience a loss.

Diversification for strategic business risk

Diversification can also be applied to reducing strategic business risk, so for example:

- selling a wide range of products to avoid dependence on any single product; or
- operating in a wide variety of markets to avoid dependence on any single market or currency

6. Treasury department and financial risk

The management of financial risk is undertaken by the treasury department. The typical roles of the treasury department include:

- Cashflow forecasting and management
- Relations with Banks
- Relations with other investors
- Working capital management
- Foreign exchange management and hedging
- Managing investments, and investment risks.

One key issue for an organisation to consider is whether the treasury department should be set up as a profit centre (where the manager in charge is incentivised to maximise profits on its dealings) or cost centre (where costs are allocated to the department and the department run within that budget).

Operating as a profit centre incentivises good investment performance and the optimum management of currencies to maximise profits for the organisation. On the downside it can also encourage risk taking by that department, in an area which is not a core expertise of the business.

In most organisations the purpose of the treasury department is to manage and control risk rather than be taking increased risks for the organisation, which is not an issue if the organisation is set up as a cost centre.

CIMA P3 Course Notes

Chapter 10
Currency Risk

1. Currency risk

Currency risk the potential change in the exchange rate of one currency against another. Investors or businesses face an exchange rate risk when they have assets or operations across national borders or if they have loans or borrowings in a foreign currency.

An exchange rate risk can result in an exchange gain as well as a loss. Greatest concern occurs when there is possibility that currency depreciation will negatively affect the value of one's assets, investments, and their related interest and dividend payment streams, especially those securities denominated in foreign currency.

There are two key types of currency risk transaction and translation risk.

2. Translation risk

Translation risk is an accounting concept. It is proportional to the amount of assets held in foreign currencies. Changes in the exchange rate over time will change the value of assets when converted back into the business' home currency.

These risks are usually mitigated by **netting** assets in that currency with by borrowings in that currency, hence reducing the net value to be translated into the home currency for financial reporting purposes.

3. Transaction risk

Transaction risk is the risk that an exchange rate will change unfavourably over time. It is associated with the **time delay between entering into a contract and settling it**. The greater the time differential between the entrance and settlement of the contract, the greater the transaction risk, because there is more time for the two exchange rates to fluctuate.

Transaction risk can be managed using the following **internal hedging techniques:**

Matching - receipts in one foreign currency are matched against payments made in the same currency, reducing the total amount that needs to be converted back into the home currency. E.g. £1m is received by a European company and those receipts used to pay a UK supplier meaning the funds never have to be converted in €. A **foreign currency bank account** can be used to hold receipts until payments are due.

Lagging - paying amounts due later to match against funds to be received in that currency or in anticipation of favourable exchange rate movements.

Leading - paying amounts due early using funds already received in that currency or in anticipation of unfavourable exchange rate movements.

Invoicing in home currency - therefore no currency risk is taken, although care should be taken since this effectively passes the risk on to customers, who may see this unfavourably.

Counter-trading - where customers are also suppliers payment could be made in goods and services.

Netting intercompany transactions - A centralised treasury department can offset payments made between divisions or subsidiaries in different countries (and hence using different currencies) to keep the total amounts exchanged to a minimum.

Internal hedging techniques like these are quick and simple and can be done within the company. There are also **external hedging** techniques which involve transactions with another party (e.g. forwards, options, futures, money market hedging). These are more complicated and we'll cover these in detail later.

4. Exchange rates terminology

Expressing exchange rates

Exchange rates are often expressed as follows:

£/€ 1.50   which means £1 = €1.50

This can also be shown another way:

€/£ 0.67 which means €1 = £0.67

Note that these two examples are exactly the same exchange rates, just shown in different ways.

Spot rate

The spot rate is the exchange rate on the day of the transaction.

Bid offer spread

This is the difference between the amount the bank will buy and sell currency at.

If the current bid price for the €/$ currency pair is 1.5760 and the current ask price is 1.5763, this means that currently you can sell the € at 1.5760 and buy at 1.5763.

The difference between those prices (3 pips) is the spread. It is effectively the profit taken by the bank.

In the exam if you are quoted a spread and are unsure which rate to use, always use the basic rule that the **'Bank always wins!'**. Always use the rate which is most favourable to the bank.

In the above example, if a US company are buying €1m. One rate would cost them $1.576m and the second $1.5763m. The worst for the company and best for the bank is the second option, so that's the rate to take!

Exchange Cross Rates

If you know the £/$ exchange rate and the £/€ exchange rate, you are then able to work out the $/€ rate. That is an 'exchange cross rate'.

So for example

$/£ : £1 = $1.50

€/£ : £1 = €1.20

From this information, the cross rate for $/€ can be calculated as follows:

$$\frac{\$/£}{€/£} = \frac{1.50}{1.20} = 1.25$$

5. Interest rate parity theory

If interest rates are higher in one country than another, you would naturally expect investors to transfer their money to a country where they can get higher interest rates. However, that process of converting money changes the exchange rate, as exchange rates relate to the supply and demand of currency in the market. i.e. if lots of people were to sell £ into € to get higher interest rates in the Euro Zone then there is an increasing supply of £ and fewer €, in the market and as such the £ will depreciate against the €.

This is known as the **Fisher effect**.

According to the **interest rate parity theory** the net effect means that the investor who moves money overseas to get higher interest rates, upon moving it back (say after a year of investment) will end up with exactly the same amount as if they had invested in their own currency as the exchange rate will have moved to exactly match the two.

To put this another way, if we take our example above, there is no benefit from investors selling their £ into € as although they'll get higher interest rates, by the time they convert it back the exchange rate has move and they'll have no more than just investing in the UK.

This works because if there is a profit to be made from such a difference in interest rates in different currencies, bankers called **'arbitragers'** will swiftly make a series of transactions to profit from it and from which it can be shown that net effect of arbitrage behaviour is that the average person has nothing to gain. Interest rate parity theory does hold out quite well in the real world therefore.

As a result the future exchange rate can be calculated based on the following formula (this is for a £/$ rate):

$$\text{Forward rate £/\$} = \text{Spot rate £/\$} \times \frac{1 + \text{US interest rate}}{1 + \text{UK interest rate}}$$

So if interest rates in the US are 4% and the UK 2%, and the current spot rate is $1 = $0.67. In 1 years time the expected future rate will be:

$$\text{Future rate £/\$} = 0.67 \times \frac{1 + 0.02}{1 + 0.04}$$

$$= 0.657$$

6. Purchasing power parity theory

Law of one price

Purchasing power parity (PPP) asks how much money would be needed to purchase the same goods and services in two countries, and uses that to calculate an implicit foreign exchange rate.

The concept is based on the (theoretical) law of one price, where in the absence of transaction costs and official trade barriers, identical goods will have the same price in different markets when the prices are expressed in the same currency. For example a car that is £10,000 in one market will be €8,000. Should that car go up to £11,000 in the UK due to inflation, exchange rates will adjust so that people in the UK can't benefit from buying in the Euro Zone as they would only get €8,000 when they do the conversion.

Like interest rate parity theory this effect is also due to arbitragers taking advantage of lower prices very quickly and buying from overseas which as a result causes exchange rates to change. In the real world there can be reasons why this is not the case, such as differing transportation costs or input costs, but the theory at least assumes that with free trade and no transactions costs there should be one single price. For these reasons Purchasing Power Parity theory holds up less well in the real world than interest rate parity theory.

Using PPP to calculate forward exchange rates

Prices change in different countries due to different inflation rates. Using the 'law of one price' the comparative prices when converted into a common currency in the future should still remain equivalent though. For this to be the case the exchange rate must change.

As a result the exchange rate can be calculated based on the following formula (this is for a £/$ rate):

Forward rate £/$ =   **Spot rate £/$**   x $\dfrac{1+\text{US inflation rate}}{1+\text{UK inflation rate}}$

So if inflation in the US is 2% and the UK 1%, and the current spot rate is $1 = £0.67
In 1 years time the expected future rate will be:

Forward rate £/$ =   0.67   x $\dfrac{1 + 0.01}{1 + 0.02}$

                =   0.663

CIMA P3 Course Notes

Chapter 11
Currency hedging techniques

1. Hedging and Transaction Risk

Managing Transaction risk

External hedging is one of the key methods of dealing with transaction risk – as a reminder, transaction risk is the risk that between the point of contract and the point of receiving or paying the funds in a foreign currency, the exchange rate will have changed and we will have to pay more or receive less expected.

We've already covered various ways of dealing with transaction risk using internal hedging techniques - can you remember these?

Let's remind you quickly.....

- **Matching** - receipts in one foreign currency are matched against payments made in the same currency, reducing the total amount that needs to be converted back into the home currency.

- **Lagging** – paying amounts due later to match against funds to be received in that currency or in anticipation of favourable exchange rate movements.

- **Leading** – paying amounts due early using funds already received in that currency or in anticipation of unfavourable exchange rate movements.

- **Invoicing in home currency** – therefore no currency risk is taken, although care should be taken since this effectively passes the risk on to customers, who may see this unfavourably.

- **Counter-trading** – where customers are also suppliers payment could be made in goods and services.

- **Netting intercompany transactions** – A centralised treasury department can offset payments made between divisions or subsidiaries in different countries (and hence using different currencies) to keep the total amounts exchanged to a minimum.

External Hedging

Let's look at a formal definition....

A hedge is an investment position intended to offset potential losses that may be incurred by a companion investment.

Let's break that definition down then – here are the constituents:

Companion investment – in our case that'll be the main transaction such as purchasing something expensive in a foreign currency

Investment position – we're undertaking some other transaction or investment in addition to the main transaction we're doing

Offset potential losses – so that should we make a loss on the original transaction, the 'investment' will counteract that

There are 5 key techniques for hedging currency risk:

- Forwards
- Money market hedge
- Futures
- Options
- Currency SWAPs

In this chapter we'll look at these techniques.

2. Forwards

What is a forward contract?

A **forward contract** or simply a forward is a non-standardised contract between two parties to buy or sell a fixed amount of foreign currency at a specified future time at a price agreed upon today.

The forward price of such a contract is commonly contrasted with the **spot price**, which is the current exchange rate.

The difference between the spot and the forward price is the forward premium or forward discount.

How a forward contract works

Generic example

Suppose that Bob wants to buy a house a year from now. At the same time, suppose that Andy currently owns a $100,000 house that he wishes to sell a year from now. Both parties could enter into a forward contract with each other. Suppose that they both agree on the sale price in one year's time of $104,000. Andy and Bob have entered into a forward contract.

Bob has now fixed the amount he will pay for this house, ensuring he never has to pay any more than $104,000. This helps him to manage his cashflows and reduce his exposure to fluctuations in the property market.

Currency example

A similar situation works for currency forwards, where one party opens a forward contract to buy or sell a currency (for example a contract to buy Euros) to expire/settle at a future date, as they do not wish to be exposed to exchange rate/currency risk over a period of time.

Sometimes, the buy forward is opened because the investor will actually need Euros at a future date such as to pay a debt owed that is denominated in Euros therefore avoiding the risk that they have to pay more due to unfavourable exchange rate movements. This is the typical use of forwards by accountants.

It is also possible that, the party opening a forward does so, not because they need Euros because they are hedging currency risk, but because they are speculating on the currency, expecting the exchange rate to move favourably to generate a gain on closing the contract.

Forwards are popular, as they are simple and flexible. Other characteristics include:

- Legally binding contract (so it must be completed even If the need for the foreign currency or amount changes)
- You set any date for exercising, but that date is set and agreed
- Agree any amount required
- Bank offers a forward exchange rate

Numerical example

The current forward price quoted for the €/$ in 6 months time is 1.5 - 1.52.

If a US company needs €1m for a contract to be paid in 6 months. Firstly we need to work out which of the two values is spread is the relevant one here. Remember - the bank always wins. One rate would cost them $1.5m and the second $1.52m. The worst for the company and best for the bank is the second option, so that's the relevant forward rate, and that's the amount payable in 6 months time.

3. Money market hedge

What is a money market hedge?

There are two types of money market hedge:

Paying in a foreign currency in the future

The home currency is converted at the spot rate, and monies held in a foreign currency bank account until required for payment in the future.

The exchange rate used was the rate now, and hence the risk of rates changing by the payment date is removed.

Receiving money in a currency in the future

A loan is taken out in a foreign currency, and that converted at the spot rate now. When the monies are received in the foreign currency they are used to pay off the foreign currency loan.

Again note that the exchange rate used was the rate now, and hence the risk of rates changing by the receipt date is removed.

Example question

ABC plc will be required to make a $2m payment in 8 months time to MacroSoft Inc. The current exchange rate is €1 = $2. The exchange rate for the $ is highly volatile.

The company's banks are willing to undertake a forward contract at a rate of €1 = $1.9.

A € loan would incur rates of interest are 10% per annum, while a $ deposit would secure a return of 13% per annum.

Compare the costs of leading (paying now), with using a future or money market hedge.

Example Solution

Payment now – Amount payable = $\frac{\$2m}{2}$ = €1m

Forward rates – Amount payable = $\frac{\$2m}{1.9}$ = €1,052,632m

Money market hedge

Steps 1 - Borrow now and convert to the currency of payment

ABC plc will **(1 in the diagram)** borrow money now in €, convert this at the spot rate to $ **(2 in the diagram)**.

Step 2 - Make the payment

This will then earn interest for 8 months when the payment can be made **(3)**.

Take a quick look at the diagram to see how this works... Note that the end effect here is that ABC has undertaken an exchange rate transaction at the spot rate (the rate now) and so has not taken any exchange rate risk. MacroSoft has received their money when they wanted it in $ so they're happy too!

	€		$
NOW	(1) Borrow 920, 245.50 and covert now to $ at €1 = $2 ⬇ Interest payable at 10% for 8 months = 6.66% ⬇	→	(2) Deposit 1,840, 491 into a $ account ⬇ This grows at 13% for 8 months – effective interest rate = 13% x 8/12 = 8.66% ⬇
8 months	(4) After 8 months the effective amount due would be 981,595		(3) Make payment of $2m

Step 3 - Work out the effective cost and exchange rate

The next step here, to work out the 'effective cost' to ABC plc....

Let's apply the € interest rate to the amount borrowed. That gives you the amount that ABC owes in € at the end of the 8 months that they now need to pay off. This is known at the 'effective cost'. **(See 4 in the diagram)**.

Even if in step 1 ABC just paid in cash and didn't borrow the money we still calculate the 'effective cost' as they've lost the equivalent amount of interest they could have earned if that money was invested for that time frame.

Note that to do the calculation you have to start with amount (3), then work out amount (2), then (1) and then (4).

Effective amount payable in 8 months is €981,595

You can also work out the **effective exchange rate**.

The 'effective' exchange rate is:

$$\frac{Actual\ Payment}{Effective\ Cost} = \frac{\$2,000,000}{€981,595} = 2.04\ \$/€$$

Conclusion

The money market hedge is the lowest cost method of hedging the risk costing €981k vs a forward which costs €1,052k.

Calculating money market hedge when receiving funds - this example is for paying a foreign currency amount. When receiving the funds, note that the same diagram is used to do the calculation and order of the calculation on the diagram (1-4) is the same, its just that you are borrowing funds in the foreign currency (rather than investing funds) and then paying off that loan with the amount foreign currency received.

4. Currency futures

What is a currency future?

A currency future is a futures contract to exchange one currency for another at a specified date in the future at a price (exchange rate) that is fixed on the purchase date.

They differ from forwards in that the contracts are **standardised amounts** (e.g. €125,000 is typical) which are **traded** on currency exchanges

Typically, one of the currencies is the US dollar. The price of a future is then in terms of US dollars per unit of other currency.

If you hold a contract at the end of the last trading day, actual payments are made in each currency. However, most contracts are closed out before that. Investors can close out the contract at any time prior to the contract's delivery date by selling it on the market.

Investors use these futures contracts to hedge against foreign exchange risk. If an investor will receive a cashflow denominated in a foreign currency on some future date, that investor can lock in the current exchange rate by entering into an offsetting currency futures position that expires on the date of the cashflow.

Further notes on how futures work:

1. Controlled by an exchange (in US) – gives security
2. Deposit required by exchange from both parties (in a client's margin account)
3. Profits and losses in the margin account are adjusted daily
4. Futures are always a standard size i.e. £62,500
5. Maturity dates are fixed at end of March, June, September and December

Futures Calculation

A UK company has to pay $240,000 on 31st May. The current spot rate is $1.9/£. Futures are sold in contract sizes of £62,500 and the current price of a future to the end of June is $1.9200/£. On 31 May, the spot rate and the futures rate on that date are both $1.8/£.

To do futures questions you can always follow the same standard steps which are as follows:

Step 1 – Work out the number of contracts needed?

Divide the total amount ($240,000) by the current futures price ($1.92) to get the £ amount needed – £125,000

Therefore 2 contracts of £62,500 are needed.

Step 2 – Are you buying or selling futures?

Use the following rule:

Owe € or £ – Buying € or £ futures

Owed € or £ – Selling € or £ futures

Owe $ – Selling € or £ futures

Owed $ – Buying € or £ futures

In this case the company owes $ so is selling futures.

Step 3 – Close out the contract (31 May)

Use the following rule:

Selling futures: opening price – closing price

Buying futures: closing price – opening price

Here we are selling futures (step 2) so take the opening price – closing price:

Opening price	$1.9200	
Closing price	$(1.8000)	
Profit/(loss)	$0.1200	which is positive so is a profit

Total profit = 2 contracts x £62,500 x $0.12 = $15,000 profit

Step 4 Undertake the spot market transaction (31 May)

Total needed	$240,000	
Less profit from future	($15,000)	(add on if step 3 is a loss)
Balance at spot rate(1.8)	**$225,000**	

In £ this is 225,000/1.8 = £125,000

5. Currency options

What is a currency option?

A currency option gives the owner the **right but not the obligation** to exchange money denominated in one currency into another currency at a pre-agreed exchange rate on a specified date.

The key is to note that there is **no obligation** to undertake the option, which gives much more flexibility to the purchaser than a forward as they can pull out of the deal if exchange rates move favourably. Of course, this increases risk to the bank and so options are more expensive.

A **premium** is the fee paid when an option is taken out.

Example

For example a £/$ contract could give the owner the right to sell £1,000,000 and buy $2,000,000 on December 31. In this case the pre-agreed exchange rate, or **strike price**, is $2 per £1 and the **notional amounts** are £1,000,000 and $2,000,000.

On the exercise date (31 December), if the spot rate is higher than 2, the option is lapsed, as it is better to take the spot rate.

If the rate is lower than 2 on December 31 (say at 1.9), meaning that the dollar is stronger and the pound is weaker, then the option is exercised, allowing the owner to sell £ at 2 and immediately buy it back in the spot market at 1.9, making a profit of:

(2 – 1.9)   x   1,000,000   = $100,000

If they immediately convert the profit into £ this amounts to 100,000/1.9000 = £52,631.58 foreign-exchange option.

Black-Scholes options pricing model

The Black-Scholes model provides a formula which can be used to price options. Many empirical tests have shown the Black-Scholes price is "fairly close" to the observed prices

You do not need to do calculations for the exam, but should know that the options price depends on the following factors:

The current price (e.g. current exchange rate) – sets the underlying value of the option. i.e. the higher the current price the higher the likely price in the future – so this is the 'base' starting point.

The strike price of the option – the more favourable the price to the buyer the more expensive the option will be as the more likely the seller will have to pay out.

The annualised risk-free interest rate - like a present value calculation; future returns need to be discounted to present value to find the current price. Like with our normal present value calculations, the higher the interest rate the lower the present value and so the lower the price.

Volatility - the greater the volatility the higher the risk to the seller so the higher the price.

Time until expiry - the longer into the future, the longer the period to be discounted and the greater the chance of a change in value of the underlying asset, increasing risk for the option seller.

6. Currency SWAPS

What is a currency SWAP?

A currency swap is where two parties agree to exchange "cash flows" with the aim of removing currency risk.

How can both parties gain from "Swapping" cashflows?

Let's say there are two people, Bob and Slavek. Bob lives in the UK and Slavek in Slovakia. Bob is buying a property in Slovakia and has to pay €100,000 in 3 months time. Slavek on the other hand is buying a business in the UK, and that's going to cost him £80,000, which, conveniently, works out at €100,000 at the current spot rate (the exchange rate right now).

Both are subject to changes in the £/€ rate of exchange - but might it be sensible here if they simply just agreed to swap their cashflows - Bob will pay Slavek's £80,000, and Slavek pays Bob's €100,000. We'll it would, of course, as then they'd completely remove the exchange rate risk. Not only that but they won't have to pay bank fees for the transaction deal either.

The key problem of course is that they now need to be able to trust each other, and they would need to agree a contract between themselves so that each party is committed to the payment. This risk of non-payment by the other party is called **'counterparty risk'**.

astranti
financial training

CIMA P3 Course Notes

Chapter 12
Interest rate risk

1. Interest rate risk

Interest rate risk is the risk of a change in interest rates on an interest-bearing asset, such as a loan or a bond.

Floating rate debt changes with market interest rates and so fluctuates with market movements, creating risk, for example if interest rates rise on a loan meaning future interest rate payments are higher.

The interest on fixed rate debt does not change, so is lower risk.

2. Hedging interest rate risk

If an organisation knows they will be taking out loans at some point in the future, and want to hedge the risk that the interest rate will change prior taking out the loan then interest rate hedging can be used.

Key types of interest rate hedge:

Forward rate agreement

A forward rate agreement (FRA) is a contract between two parties that determines the rate of interest to be paid or received on an obligation beginning at a future start date. (It is similar in nature to a currency forward, but for interest rates). The contract will determine the rates to be used along with the termination date and notional value.

On this type of agreement, it is only the differential that is paid on the notional amount of the contract, so for instance if rates rise by 1% between taking out the FRA and the date when the actual loan is taken out, then the company takes out the loan at the higher rate, but is able to recoup the additional 1% interest from the party with whom the FRA was taken out.

You are not required to undertake calculations on FRAs in the exam.

Interest rate guarantees (IRG)

An interest rate guarantee (IRG) is an option on a forward rate agreement (FRA) that is agreed between two parties (e.g. the company and a bank).

When exercising an IRG, the holder has the option (but is not obliged) to take a loan of a predetermined amount at a predetermined interest rate for a predetermined time period.

This is similar to a currency option, and enables the company (at a cost) to remove the downside risk of rates rising, while benefiting from interest rate falls.

An up front fee called a premium is paid when an IRG is taken out.

No calculations are required.

Interest rate futures

An interest rate future is an exchange traded agreement that determines the rate of interest, to be paid or received on an obligation beginning at a future start date. It is similar in nature to a currency future.

Key characteristics:

- An exchange traded FRA (which gives security that the counterparty will fulfil their obligations)
- Standard amounts
- Sit alongside the actual loan (like currency futures)
- Borrowers sell futures to hedge against an increase in rates.

No calculations are required for interest rate futures in the exam.

Interest rate options

An interest rate option grants the buyer the right but not the obligation to deal in interest rate futures. It is therefore exchange traded.

A premium is payable.

No calculations are required for interest rate options in the exam.

Summary of interest rate hedging techniques

	Over The Counter (i.e. agreed directly with the bank)	Exchange traded
Fixing instruments	Forward Rate Agreement	Interest Rate Futures
Insurance instruments (right but not obligation)	Interest Rate Guarantees	Interest Rate Options

3. Interest rate SWAPS

What is an interest rate SWAP?

An interest rate swap is where two parties agree to exchange interest rate cash flows for mutual benefit.

The contract will be based on a specified notional amount from a fixed rate to a floating rate (or vice versa) or from one floating rate to another.

How can both parties gain from "Swapping" loans?

An example of a SWAP in its simplest form would be if one party can get low rates of interest on floating rate loans (but want fixed) while another party can get low rates on fixed rate loans (but want floating), so by taking out the loan they can get cheaply and 'swapping it' by effectively paying each other's interest payments, then both parties can gain.

How does it work?

The most common interest rate swap is one where one counterparty A pays a fixed rate (the swap rate) to counterparty B, while receiving a floating rate.

The floating rate is usually referred to compared to a reference rate (such as LIBOR or EURIBOR) e.g. LIBOR + 3%. If the current LIBOR rate is 2% then the payment is 5%. The LIBOR (**London Interbank Offered Rate**) is the average interest rate estimated by leading banks in London that they would be charged if borrowing from other banks.

Example

Currently, A borrows from Market @ LIBOR +1.5% (floating) or fixed of 10%. B borrows from Market @ 8.5% (fixed) or floating of LIBOR + 1%.

A wants a fixed rate, B wants a floating rate.

Together both could borrow individually for a total of 10% + LIBOR + 1% = **LIBOR +11%**

If they 'borrowed for each other' the total amount payable to banks would be LIBOR + 1.5% + 8.5% = **LIBOR + 10%.**

There is therefore a 1% saving to be made if each party can come to a suitable agreement on how to share the saving.

If we consider the following swap in which Party A takes out a floating rate loan of LIBOR + 1.5%, agrees to pay Party B periodic fixed interest rate payments of 8.65%.

Party B takes out a fixed rate loan at 8.5% and pays A LIBOR + 0.70% in the same currency. The following diagram shows the net position.

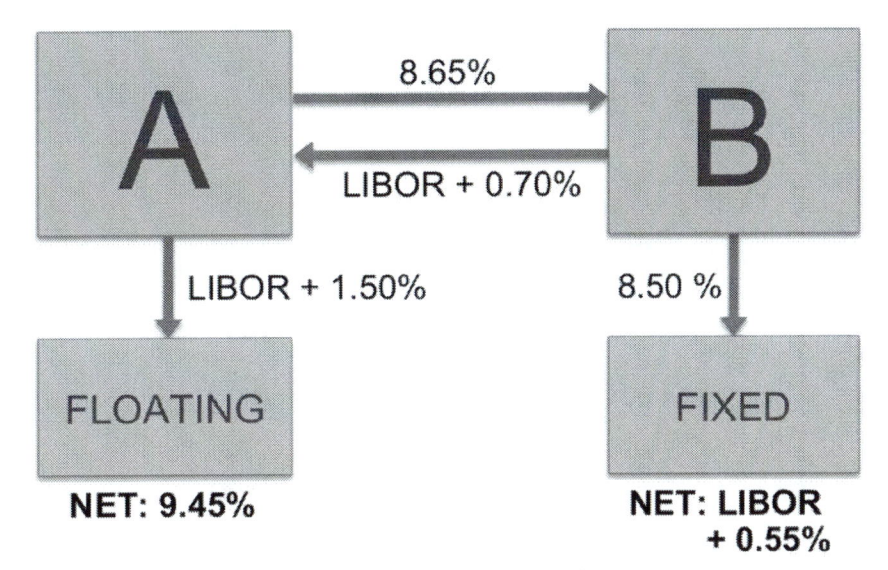

```
                8.65%
    ┌───┐ ─────────────────► ┌───┐
    │ A │                    │ B │
    └───┘ ◄───────────────── └───┘
              LIBOR + 0.70%
      │                         │
      │ LIBOR + 1.50%           │ 8.50%
      ▼                         ▼
  ┌────────┐                ┌───────┐
  │FLOATING│                │ FIXED │
  └────────┘                └───────┘
  NET: 9.45%              NET: LIBOR
                              + 0.55%
```

Party A pays (LIBOR + 1.50%)+8.65% - (LIBOR+0.70%) = 9.45% net

This is a saving of 0.55% compared with taking out the fixed rate themselves.

Party B pays 8.5% + LIBOR +0.7%- 8.65% = LIBOR + 0.55% net

This is a saving of 0.45% compared with taking out the floating rate alone.

You DO need to be able to calculations like this in the exam!

Advantages

- May reduce total borrowing costs
- Flexible – up to the two parties to agree terms
- Can be used to foreign finance where one party may find it difficult to obtain
- Transaction costs are limited
- Able to convert floating to fixed rate loans if that's what the company wants

Disadvantages

- Professional help required (and they will charge a fee)
- Counterpart risk (i.e. the other party does not meet their obligations under the contract)
- Complex arrangements

4. Caps, Floors and Collars

An interest rate cap is a derivative in which the buyer receives payments at the end of each period in which the interest rate exceeds the agreed strike price. An example of a cap would be an agreement to receive a payment for each month the LIBOR rate exceeds 2.5%.

Similarly an interest rate floor is a derivative contract in which the buyer receives payments and seller pays them at the end of each period in which the interest rate is below the agreed strike price (e.g. 1%).

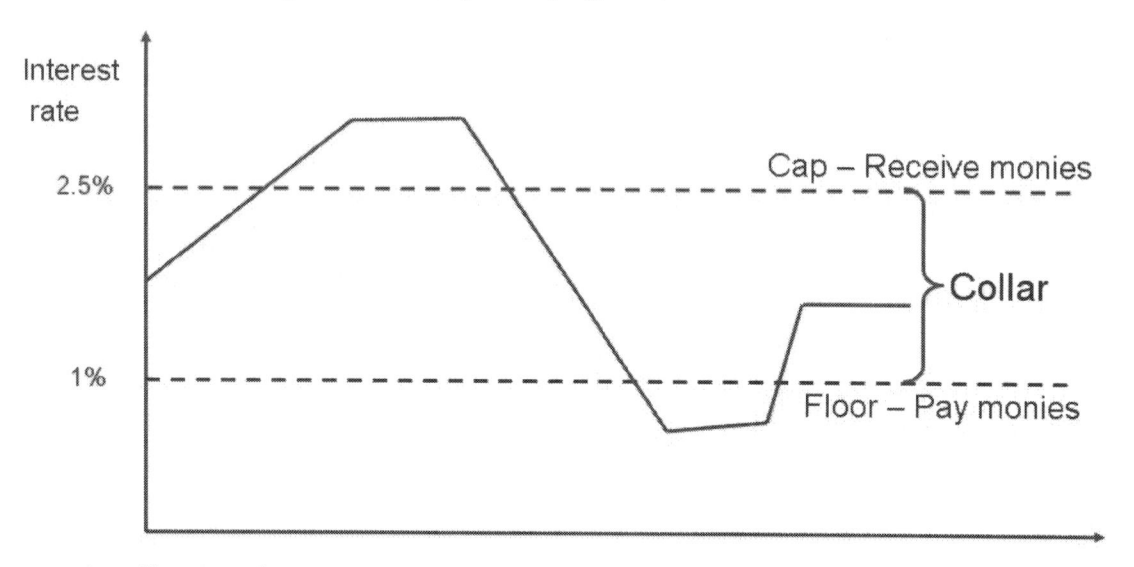

A collar combines a cap and a floor. The borrower buyers a cap, and sells a floor. To a borrower, by receiving a premium on the floor, that reduces the price paid for the premium paid on the cap, making a collar cheaper, but also not letting the borrower benefit when interest rates fall.

CIMA P3 Course Notes

Chapter 13
Investment Appraisal Risk

1. Investment appraisal risks

Evaluating Investment decisions

Before new investments are made, for example in new technology, buildings or even a new business opportunity, a financial appraisal of that investment supports the decision making process, by providing an objective and robust analysis of whether the project should proceed.

From a financial perspective we use techniques such as Net Present Value (NPV), Internal rate of return (IRR), Payback period and Return on capital employed (ROCE) to help our decision making process, with the NPV typically being recognised as the best method of evaluation as it considers all the future cashflows discounted at the company's cost of capital. A positive NPV means that the shareholders will get a return higher than their cost of capital and any such project should be invested in, subject to the other non-financial factors being favourable too.

Risks in investment analysis

Intrinsic in the calculation of the NPV is the company's cost of capital – the average of the cost of debt and equity.

There are some risks associated with using the cost of capital figure though:

- Debt levels and interest can change over time and so the cost of capital over the duration of the project may be uncertain.

- Shareholder's required returns can vary depending on factors such as the economy, the stock market performance, and interest rates again meaning the cost of capital may vary.

- Often it is hard to calculate an accurate cost of capital – the relevant information simply is not available, particularly for the cost of equity (what return do shareholders really want? Often even they don't know themselves!). The cost of capital figure therefore is often just an estimate.

- Often the weighted average of the debt and equity (the WACC) is used to appraise investments, but that does not take into account how the investment will be funded. For instance a safe investment funded through a large amount of cheap secured debt could reduce the average cost of capital.

- It assumes that the project being evaluated is at the same risk level as the company as a whole.

That last point is a key one to dwell upon for a moment – what does that mean? Well, let's say we were a well established bread manufacturer in a nice, safe stable business that had very consistent profits year after year due to the respected brand and nature of the product as a key necessity. Our cost of capital is likely to be relatively low due to the low risk business we are in. What if we were to branch out into a new field such as space travel? (That may sound far fetched but it's exactly what Virgin have done!). Well space travel is hugely risky. It would be crazy to use the same cost of capital figure that we currently have for our stable, steady and safe bread business to evaluate our new space travel business; a much higher one is needed.

The second element of the NPV calculation is the future estimated cashflows. The risks there can include:

- Initial future cashflows are usually just estimates – often the best guess of the accounting and business teams.

- Changes in external factors such as economic growth, interest rates, changing customer demands, new technology or competitor actions can make even the best estimates unravel in real world operations.

So the question comes then – how can we deal with these 'investment appraisal risks'. Well there are a number of methods – and we'll be taking a look at some of them in this chapter.

Conflicts and investment decisions

Stakeholder conflict

Different stakeholders will have different views on a particular investment – some will want lower risks (staff for instance who simply want to retain their job, or a bank who want to guarantee return of their loans), while others may want higher risks taken (risk seeking shareholders for instance, who want high, short term returns)

Stakeholder management is therefore key for significant investment decisions. That includes wide consultation and communication with all key stakeholders affected by the decision both prior to the decision itself and during the investment process.

Profit Maximisation vs Wealth Maximisation

One regular investment conflict is between:

- **maximising short term profits**, often gained through keeping costs low in the short term, and investing only in projects with high short term returns giving higher ROCE.

- and, **maximising wealth** – wealth is maximised by the highest NPV projects as the NPV of a project is effectively an estimate of the increase in value of the company if the project were to go ahead.

Often these two objectives are consistent, but when a project has high returns in the long term where returns do not arise for a number of years, then the NPV could be high, but profits could be lower for the next few years due to the costs involved in getting the project up and running.

In theory wealth maximisation should be the goal of an organisation making investment decisions, but in the real world short term targets imposed on directors and investment managers mean that the shorter term profit goals could become the focus.

2. Sensitivity Analysis

Sensitivity analysis allows us to consider the impact that a change in one variable, for example revenue, would need to be for the NPV of a project to fall to 0.

When we are calculating future revenue, however good our assumptions are, this is only a best guess as unforeseeable events could easily make this forecast irrelevant. What sensitivity analysis considers is how much flex we have in a particular factor before we start losing money. Would it require a 20% drop to our revenue forecast or a 2% drop?

It is another way of testing the robustness of a project.

$$\text{Sensitivity Analysis} = \frac{\text{NPV of project}}{\text{PV of one variable (e.g. sales)}}$$

Example

Let's consider a project with an NPV of £167.59 with an asset we can sell in year 5 for £525. The question is, how sensitive is the NPV to the change in disposal value? Put another way, how much lower would the disposal value have to be before the project is not viable?

The cost of capital is 12%.

Solution

Note that the first step is to work out the PV of the asset disposal figure (525 x 0.567), and then applying the formula.

The answer of 56% means that the disposal value can fall by 56% (or £166.70) before the project becomes unviable.

We can then look at the market for the asset and any likely changes in that market to decide whether this is likely or not. If there is a liquid market and the prices are typically stable then there would appear to be a small likelihood the value would fall this far and we could proceed with the project. If prices are highly variable and we have great uncertainty in final prices we may decide the project is too risky.

Multiple variables

In a larger project you can calculate the sensitivity to a variety of different variables and then assess the likelihood that each will vary to a certain degree.

Do note though that a limit of this analysis is that it only considers one variable at a time. If two or three variables changed adversely at the same time the affect would be severe on the NPV, but this would not necessarily be seen in any single figure. Fore example if prices fell by 10%, costs rose by 15% and the final resale value fell by 20% - the combined effect of these changes would be significant, and not clearly demonstrated in any single sensitivity figure calculated.

3. Certainty Equivalents

Certainty equivalents are a way of adjusting a project's cash flows to allow for risk in an investment appraisal. Project cash flows are converted to **riskless equivalents**, the greater the risk the smaller the equivalent value.

For example, an amusement park, might expect annual revenues on a new ride to be €100,000, but know there is some variability in those revenues depending on weather. Based on many years of past data, they know that in the worst years revenues are 35% lower. We can therefore apply a factor of 0.35 to the cashflow as a 'certain risk free' amount (i.e.(100%-35%) x €100,000 = €65,000)

The disadvantage of this approach is that the size of the adjustment to each cash flow is decided subjectively by management. If the amusement park above had many years of historical data to use, those adjustments may be quite accurate, but for projects that are new (e.g. sales of a brand new technology), it could be very hard to calculate accurately.

Risk-free cost of capital

The normal cost of capital used in calculations already has some risk build into it – the more risky the business the higher the cost of capital will be. However in this case we are using "riskless" cashflows which are deemed guaranteed or "certain" and so we need to use a different cost of capital - that being the "risk free rate".

Example

David's Cars are considering a project to expand their fleet, with the following expected cash flows:

	Year 0	Year 1	Year 2	Year 3
Cash flow	-10,000	8,000	5,000	3,000
Discount factor	1	0.893	0.797	0.712
PV	-10,000	7,144	3,985	2,136

NPV 3,265

The project has a positive NPV and therefore should be considered a positive option for the company.

However management do not feel that cash flow revenue can be guaranteed and want to reduce them to "certain equivalent cash flows" by taking only 75%, 60% and 50% of years 1, 2, 3.

With these deductions the remaining cash flows would be considered certain and therefore risk free. We would therefore use a risk free cost of capital rate as our discount factor for the NPV calculation. In this scenario the risk free rate is 5%.

	Year 0	Year 1	Year 2	Year 3
Cash flow	-10,000	8,000	5,000	3,000
Certainty equivalents	1.00	0.75	0.60	0.5
Discount factor @ 5%	1	0.952	0.907	0.864
PV	-10,000	5,712	2,721	1,296

NPV -115

Having reviewed the profitability of this project taking only the cash flows that the company consider to be certain, the project would appear too risky and should be rejected.

4. Diversification and systematic risk

Diversification for investment risk

Diversification is a key way of reducing investment risk. In finance, diversification means reducing risk by investing in a variety of shares, loans or other assets. This has the affect of avoiding exposure to losses on any single investment.

The simplest example of diversification is provided by the proverb "Don't put all your eggs in one basket". Dropping the basket will break all the eggs. Placing each egg in a different basket is more diversified. There is more risk of losing one egg, but less risk of losing all of them.

In finance, an example of an undiversified portfolio is to hold shares in only one company – risking everything on that company which could potentially fail. By holding a portfolio of shares in different companies in different industries means that even if one of those should do poorly it will be balanced against others that do well.

Further diversification can be obtained by investing in stocks from different countries, and in different asset classes such as bonds, property, private equity, infrastructure and commodities such as heating oil or gold. The wider the variety of the investment portfolio the less they depend on each other and the greater the diversification.

Any risk-averse investor will diversify to at least some extent, with more risk-averse investors diversifying more completely than less risk-averse investors which many investors see as an attractive prospect, so that Index Funds have been developed that invest in equities in proportion to the weighting they have in some well known index such as the FTSE.

Diversification does not eliminate the risk that all assets will move in the same direction however. During recessionary times, the whole market for shares tends to fall, so however well an investor is diversified in different types of shares they will still experience a loss.

Unsystematic risk

Risk that can be reduced using diversification is called **unsystematic risk**.

When considering returns required by investors, unsystematic risk does not need to be accounted for since it can be removed, and it is normally assumed that any rational investor will be diversified and so does not need to account for unsystematic risk.

Systematic risk

Diversification does not eliminate all the risk associated with holding securities, as there are variables that cause all assets will move in the same direction. For example, during recessionary times, the whole market for shares tends to fall, so however well an investor is diversified in different types of shares they will still experience a loss. This risk is known as **systematic risk**.

5. Capital asset pricing model

When considering returns required by investors, systematic risk must be considered as it can not be diversified away.

If the risk free rate is the rate required by investors taking no risk (often associated with the risk of highly secure government bonds where risks are minimal), then investors will therefore want a return above the systematic risk.

Depending on their nature different shares can have different levels of systematic risk, perhaps due to the industry they are in. The level of systematic risk taken by a particular asset is measured by its **Beta factor**. This is a measure of systematic risk as compared with the average for the market as a whole. Less than 1 means that share has lower risk than the market, greater than 1, means it has higher risk.

For example, in April 2012 Apple had a beta of 1.2 meaning risk was slightly higher than the market average, whereas Walmart had a beta of just 0.3 reflecting the fact that supermarkets have stable revenues even despite other economic and market changes.

The level of return required by shareholders (or the cost of equity capital) can thus be measured using the following formula:

$$k_e = R_f + [R_m - R_f]\beta$$

Ke = cost of equity capital

Rf = rate of return on a risk free investment

Rm = rate of return on the market as an average

β = Beta factor

Calculating the cost of capital for NPVs

Earlier we raised the issue of investing in projects in industries which have a different level of risk than our own industry. Remember the example of the bread company investing in space travel! Different risk levels should require different cost of capital figures to appraise the investment.

When calculating cost of capital figures for investment projects in industries other than the company's own, beta's can be a useful way of working out what cost of capital to use. Let's see how.

Example

A company is aiming to calculate their required return for an investment project in a new industry, a supermarket group of which a typical beta is 0.3. The current return of government bonds (considered risk free) is 3%, whilst the market average return is 8%. What is the required cost of capital.

$$k_e = R_f + [R_m - R_f]\beta$$

= 3% + [8%-3%] x 0.3

= 4.5%

Betas and financial risk

As well as being susceptible to systematic risk, betas also change depending on the level of gearing in a company where there is also financial risk. The higher the gearing, the greater the financial risk, and so a highly geared company will have a higher beta.

An **asset beta** (βa) is the beta of the company **without any debt**.

An **equity beta** (βe) is the beta of the company **including any debt it has**

When we know the asset beta, and debt is included in the structure of a business then we can work out the new equity beta B_e of the firm using the formula:

$$\beta e = \beta a \left(1 + \frac{D(1-t)}{E}\right)$$

D = Market value or percentage of Debt

E = Market value of percentage of Equity

t = tax rate (as a decimal)

The same formula can also be used to work out the appropriate cost of capital to use for NPV calculations for investments in **new industries** where the company will be using **different levels of debt compared to the existing company**.

Example

ABC is an all equity financed company in the supermarket industry. It has no debt. It is looking to buy a company in the clothing retailing industry. The B_e of a firm to be acquired is 1.4 and it currently has 30% debt. What is a suitable discount rate to appraise the investment of the clothing retailer if the retailer is purchased with all equity finance?

Rm = 8%, Rf = 5% and t = 30%.

Solution

The current beta of 1.4 includes some financial risk due to the levels of debt in the company, but since ABC will not be using any debt, this is not the relevant beta to them. Instead they must calculate the asset beta and use that instead.

Step 1 - Ungearing the beta

$$\beta e = \beta a \left(1 + \frac{D(1-t)}{E}\right)$$

$$1.4 = \beta a \left(1 + \frac{30\%(1-0.3)}{70\%}\right)$$

$$1.4 = \beta a \times (1 + 0.3)$$

$$\beta a = 1.08$$

This process is called 'ungearing' the beta.

Step 2 – Calculating the required cost of capital

The standard beta formula can now be used using the 'ungeared' asset beta

$$k_e = R_f + [R_m - R_f]\beta$$

= 5% + [8% - 5%] x 1.08

= 8.24%

6. Adjusted present value

Use of Weighted Average Cost of Capital

It is typical in Net Present Value calculations to use the company's weighted average cost of capital (WACC) as the cost of capital to be used to appraise projects. This ensures any new project being appraised will give a return that both covers the cost of debt and equity finance.

Adjusted present value

Where loan finance is utilised to fund a specific investment this will invariably mean that investment having a different cost of capital than the company's current weighted average cost of capital (WACC). If, for example, a company takes out a very expensive bridging loan to make a project viable, using the WACC that takes into account all of the company's financial activities would not fairly reflect the viability of this specific project.

The Adjusted Present Value calculation is a method that takes account of the project specific finance used.

The APV calculation, rather than simply taking the company's WACC allows an adjustment to be made so that the cost of capital better reflects the finances in place for the project therefore building in project specific finance to the cost of capital used to calculate the viability of a project.

In our example, being able to build in the cost of that bridging loan to create a project cost of capital, gives a much fairer reflection of profitability.

The APV calculation enables us to build project specific finance into NPV calculations and has a two stage method:

Stage 1. Evaluate the project as if it was all equity financed - this will give a 'base case NPV'.

Stage 2. Adjust calculation to reflect the financing used for this project.

Doing an APV can be complicated - they key to success is learning the process and following through that process in questions. Here's an example:

Question

Krober plc is investing £14m in a project that will yield £3.8m per annum post tax, for the next 5 years.

The project will increase Krober's debt by £10.4m for the duration of the project at an interest rate of 6%. The costs of raising this loan are estimated at £260,000 (net of tax).

The risk free rate is 5%, the market rate is 14%, the equity beta of Krober is 1.3, and corporation tax is 30%. Krober currently has a ratio of 1:1 for market value of debt to market value of equity.

Calculate and comment on the APV.

Stage 1. Finding the Base case NPV

1. Calculate an asset beta

The current beta is based on Krobner's current levels of debt (Vd) and equity (Ve). We firstly need to adjust this beta to calculate an asset beta (which is independent of current debt levels).

$$\text{Asset beta } (\beta u) = \beta g \times \frac{Vd}{Ve + Vd(1-t)} = 1.3 \times [1/(1+1\times(1-0.7))] = 0.765$$

In the question we are only told the ratio of debt to equity, so we assume Vd is 1, and Ve is also 1.

2. Calculate the ungeared cost of equity capital

Next we need to calcuate the ungeared cost of equity captial (Ke) which we will use to calculate the NPV of the project as if ungeared.

$$\text{Ke ungeared} = Ke - Rf + (Rm-Rf)\beta = 5 + (14 - 5) \times 0.76 = 11.885$$

From this calcualtion we should use 12% as the discount rate for the NPV.

3. Calculate the NPV using the ungeared cost of equity capital

Base case NPV (£m)

	Time	0	1-5	
	Cashflows	-14	3.8	
Discount factor 12%			3.605	
	PV	-14	13.699	-0.301

Based on our initial calculation the NPV of this project is negative and this project should not therefore be pursued.

Stage 2. Adjustment for the financing procured for this project

The new debt taken out has the benefit of a tax shield, so we firstly calculate that benefit:

Calculate the interest payable on the debt: 10,400,000 * 6% = £624,000

The tax saved will be   £624,000 x 30% =   £187,200

Discount at cost of debt of 6% over five years = 4.212 (see tables)
PV of tax shield   (4.212 x £187,200) =   £0.788m

To calculate the Adjusted Present value we then take our calculated NPV, add back the benefit we will get from the tax shield and deduct from this the cost of issuing the debt.

APV (£m) = -0.301 + 0.788 - 0.260 = £0.23m

Adjusting the present value to take account of the project specific cost of capital now means that we get a positive APV and that this project should be accepted.

7. Project implementation and review

Project implementation

During the implementation of a new project risks should be managed using project management planning tools such as:

- Project risk register
- Project plans using network charts or Gantt charts
- Plan review and updates
- Project reporting
- Budgeting and variance analysis
- Oversight by a project steering committee/project board

Post-implementation project reviews/audits

At the end of major projects, the final step is to review the effectiveness of the project and learn lessons to apply to future projects. While often this is carried out by the project manager, sometimes the internal audit team take part in this review as it helps bring independence to the assessment.

astranti
financial training

Objective Test Question Packs

Objective tests linked to the Study Texts on a chapter by chapter basis – practise CIMA exam style questions as you complete each chapter of the text

Mock Exam Objective Tests

Mock Exams Tests designed to emulate the 2015 CIMA exams
Perfect exam practise!

Video Tuition Guides

Comprehensive online tuition videos teaching you the full exam syllabus in a clear, concise and understandable manner

Case Study Exam Courses

Join our **online courses** for the operational, managerial and strategic case study exams including:

2 Full Day Interactive online **Masterclasses** to support and focus your study
Full course notes
Course videos – You full guide to passing the case study exams
Exam technique video guide – designed to maximise your marks
Video analysis of the latest **Preseen Case Study**
3 full, **computer-based mock exams** based around the **latest preseen** and designed to emulate the real CIMA computer exams
Marking and with detailed feedback from our team of experienced markers
Student forum so our expert case study teams can answer all your questions

All with our unique **pass guarantee scheme**

Or buy any element of the course individually – it's up to you!

Find out more at www.astranti.com

Printed in Great Britain
by Amazon.co.uk, Ltd.,
Marston Gate.